THE GLOBALIZATION OF TERRORISM

This book is dedicated with eternal love and respect to the memories of my mother and father. May their souls rest in perfect peace.

The Globalization of Terrorism

IHEKWOABA D. ONWUDIWE
University of Maryland Eastern Shore, USA

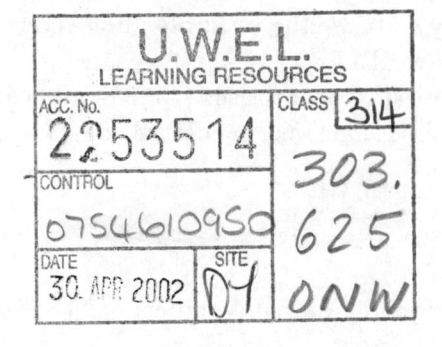
Ashgate

Published by
Ashgate Publishing Limited
Gower House
Croft Road
Aldershot
Hampshire GU11 3HR
England

Ashgate Publishing Company
131 Main Street
Burlington, VT 05401-5600 USA

Ashgate website: http://www.ashgate.com

British Library Cataloguing in Publication Data
Onwudiwe, Ihekwoaba D.
    The globalization of terrorism. - (Interdisciplinary
    research series in ethnic, gender and class relations)
    1. Terrorism
    I. Title
    303.6'25

Library of Congress Control Number: 00-133620

ISBN 0 7546 1095 0

Reprinted 2002

Printed in Great Britain by
Antony Rowe Ltd, Chippenham, Wiltshire

Table of Contents

List of Tables

Foreword

Michael J. Lynch
(Associate Professor and Director,
Ph.D. Program in Criminology
University of South Florida
Soc-107
Tampa, Florida 33620-8100
813-974-8148)

It is my great honor to be able to write a foreword for Professor Onwudiwe's book for two reasons. First, the ideas contained in this book are nothing short of a ground-breaking effort in the study of terrorism, and I shall have more to say about this below. Second, and the point I will focus on first, is the special place Professor Onwudiwe holds in my own development as a professor.

I have known Professor Onwudiwe for slightly more than a decade. During that time period I have seen him mature academically as he proceeded through his course work at Florida State University, where I served as his mentor, and directed his master's paper and doctoral dissertation. Professor Onwudiwe holds a special place in my life serving, so to speak, the role of guinea-pig as my first masters student and one of my first two doctoral students. He now also holds the distinction as being my first student to publish a book. All told, he has done well as an academic, and I am proud to have been able to serve some small role (possibly) in this development.

The first time I met Professor Onwudiwe I "butchered" his name badly, and he kindly responded in his deep, mild mannered voice, "Just call me Declan," a quick reference to his anglocized name. My first impression was that he was an impressive young man, well-mannered, intelligent, likeable, well read and astute. I can make no claim to have developed these attributes in him, as he was also academically independent, and an avaricious reader. In any event, I noticed that his previous training in political science gave him a perspective on crime and the criminal justice system that was broader than many of the graduate students one encounters in a school or department of criminal justice. His prior training caused him to look at problems of crime and justice differently than most, and this perspective is reflected in the pages that follow. His willingness and ability to view crime and justice in a different light is what sets his view of terrorism apart from the more ordinary treatments of this topic more typically encountered when reading the literature on terrorism.

Generally, the study of terrorism is undertaken from a policy perspective. That is, the majority of works on this topic offer methods for controlling terrorism. Such an approach puts the cart before the horse. In order to develop sound policies for controlling this or any other form of behavior, we must first possess a greater understanding of the causes of the behavior in question. This position is precisely the perspective that Professor Onwudiwe takes up in this book. What are the causes of terrorism? And how can terrorism be explained? These things must be known before we will be able to control terrorism.

Existing explanations of terrorism have typically been of two types. The first depicts terrorists as political actors who respond to unjust conditions. This depiction has been developed in several different directions, and sometimes evolves into descriptions that elevate terrorists to the status of heroes (which they may be at times) or revolutionaries. These descriptions have important cultural significance, and many parallels can be drawn between terrorists and the bandits described by Eric Hobwsbawm in his book that goes by the same name (*Bandits*, 1981). In any event, this view requires that we examine the ideological motivations behind terrorism and connect these to broader issues of culture and politics. This view also raises the need to examine the legitimacy of terrorists, or to determine whether terrorists have indeed taken up struggles that represent attempts to rectify broader cultural, social and political conditions related to injustice and oppression. Terrorists who fit these criteria, then, have some legitimate basis for their action, and can often be described as "freedom fighters." Terrorists be elevated to this lofty status. Their behavior is described by the second who do not fit this description, who simply have "personal agendas," cannot general view in which they are seen as little more than glorified criminals who commit unjustified and abhorrent acts of violence.

Professor Onwudiwe's book goes beyond this ordinary depiction of terrorists in his attempt to explain the pattern of terrorism seen across the face of the globe. Because of this, I think this is a book that anyone interested in terrorism must read and grapple with, for assuredly, it contains answers we might otherwise overlook or even avoid. Clearly, this book contains a perspective no one else has applied to terrorism.

Rather than focus on terrorists and the attempt to classify them as freedom fighters or criminals, Professor Onwudiwe looks at terrorism as the consequence of how the world is ordered. To do so, he employs world systems theory as the background for his analysis of terrorist incidents across numerous nations, and in his case studies of African nations. Briefly, we can describe world systems theory as a model of world order that views the nations of the world as elements in a broader system tied together by economic and political relationships. The world order, in other words, has a structural dimension dictated by relationships that exist among nations on both the economic and political levels. Within the global world order, nations, in effect, occupy position similar to the class locations individuals occupy within nations. There are dominant nations that control world resources and manufacturing practices, and which possess the ability to translate their economic resources into political and military strength used to maintain a world order that continues to benefit their best interests. World systems theorists argue that these controlling nations, what they call the core nations, are composed primarily of the leading capitalist nations of the world. These nations are "leaders" in the economic realm (they are "leaders" to the extent that they are the owners of the primary means of economic production, and to the extent that they control global resources and wealth), control numerous treaties and act as protectorates for other nations, and can employ their economic powers to shape domestic and international issues across the face of the globe. In addition, they have the military might to enforce their will when challenged. I will side-step a description of the nations in the middle of the world system -- the semi-peripheral nations -- to get more directly to the broader point.

At the bottom of the world hierarchy are the peripheral nations. These nations possess few economic resources with respect to manufacturing. The resources these nations do possess, often reflected in a wealth of natural resources, are needed to operate the economic machinery owned by those living in core nations. The core, in other words, has economic interests in protecting the periphery from interventions that would disrupt the ability of core manufacturers to exploit the natural resource as well as the cheap labor found in peripheral nations. In short, the world system is a class model that depends upon the continued existence of inequality and exploitation as the basis of its existence. This is the context against which Professor Onwudiwe examines patterns of terrorism.

Professor Onwudiwe's data on terrorist incidents indicates several important trends. First, the majority of terrorist actions are committed against core nation targets. Second, the majority of terrorist incidents occur in peripheral nations. Third, while terrorism is more prevalent in the periphery, the nation most often targeted by terrorist incidents, the U.S., is viewed as the most influential core nation. Each of these outcomes fits well with the expectations or hypotheses Professor Onwudiwe derives from world systems theory. To flesh out these patterns and their meanings, Professor Onwudiwe employs several nation specific case studies which also support the idea that patterns of terrorism are strongly influenced by the nature of the capitalist world economic system. Professor Onwudiwe's analysis is enlightening and important for its unique, well-argued, well-documented, and well-thought out view. One of the more interesting aspects of his approach has to do with a point mentioned above, namely, the response to terrorism. Rather than spend an extensive amount of time reviewing the materials that support Professor Onwudiwe's interpretation of terrorism which can be found in the following pages, I will move on to a further discussion of this study's implications, for these are, in their own right, fascinating.

The implications of Professor Onwudiwe's study are numerous, and many are examined throughout the text which follows. The most important of these relates to the control of terrorism. If terrorism is, as Professor Ownudiwe suggests, a response to the structure of the world system -- a response to the global inequality that exists between nations -- the only solutions that will have any significant impact on the reduction and control of terrorism are those that restructure the world; that is, policies that eliminate cross-national inequality and existing patterns of exploitation that extend from the core to the peripheral nations of the world. Military interventions, attempts at "target hardening," or other forms of social control such as economic sanctions, may work in the short run to contain terrorism, but only temporarily. In the long run, however, these policies have been and will continue to be ineffective since they do nothing to remedy the conditions that set the stage for terrorism: namely, global inequality. More importantly, in a system of global inequality and exploitation, attempts to control terrorism -- actions generally undertaken by the core and directed at peripheral and semi-peripheral nations -- simply serve as further evidence of inequality and oppression to those who already occupy the position of the oppressed in peripheral nations. The extension of control by the core, in other words, is simply seen as more of the same by those who initiate terrorism, and terrorists have developed mechanisms for converting these attempts at control into evidence that justified a continuation of their actions (e.g., Saddam Hussein). Control responses, in essence, become further aggravating circumstances that keep the cycle of violence characteristic of terrorism in motion. Below, I put my own twist on this finding.

Most assuredly, the elimination of global forms of inequality that would end terrorism is a tall order. And many will view this idea as an ideal -- a fanciful utopian international society -- that cannot be accomplished. The history of the world is, after all, the history of nations imposing their wills against one another in an effort to establish domination and to benefit from exploitive relationships. Nevertheless, what Professor Onwudiwe's careful analysis points towards is that we must continue to expect terrorist actions to occur as long as the nations of the world exist in an international web of interdependency characterized by inequality and oppression. In other words, to expect terrorism to disappear in a world based upon inequality -- or to be able to crush it out -- is no less of a pipe-dream than is a world based upon equality. Thus, we are left with choosing between two paths: the attempt to eliminate inequality between nations, or the attempt to employ power in the attempt to suppress expressions of dissatisfaction with inequality. The first position may never be achieved; but, then, neither will the second. In short, the choice comes down to selecting the more peaceful and idealistic path, or the more violent and destructive path. This second, more destructive path, which we have traveled down many times before, only assures us that terrorism will continue to flourish across the face of the globe. The challenge is to select the path to peace rather than the pathway of continued oppression. Human history is marred by our continued choice of the pathway to oppression, the violence that attempts to maintain these forms of oppression, and is littered with the human bodies these violent responses has consumed. So, shall it be more of the same? Or will we comprehend that inequality breeds the violence that terrorism expresses and develop a new reaction? Only the unfolding of human history can tell the story of our choice.

In closing, let me reiterate that I believe that Professor Onwudiwe has produced a truly outstanding work on terrorism that is to be respected for its unique interpretive position. It is, to be sure, a work that must be read and addressed by those interested in terrorism.

Series Editor's Preface

The work of Professor Ihekwoaba Onwudiwe is a welcome addition to the Ashgate Interdisciplinary Research Series in Ethnic, Gender and Class Relations. He mentioned this work to me after the lunch of the Division on Peoples of Color at the American Society of Criminology meeting in San Diego. During the round of introductions, I had announced to the members present that I edit this series and that if they have a manuscript, they should send me a proposal. However, to my amazement, someone else stood up to say that my series would have to compete against her series on a university press for the limited supply of good manuscripts. I told her that the more avenues open for the publication of critical work that would otherwise be rejected for not fitting in, the better, as far as I was concerned. I am pleased that Dr Onwudiwe chose to publish this important work in this series.

I was intrigued by Dr Onwudiwe's use of World System Theory (WST) to explain global terrorism and we discussed his work as an African resident of San Diego offered to give us a ride across to Tijuana in Mexico before our departure. On that trip, evidence of the WST was everywhere before us. For example, there was no immigration check on the Mexico side where the poorer government was only too glad to have us come and spend our welcome dollars in their economy. However, on our return to San Diego that day, the queue to the border control was very long and when we eventually got there, the uniformed official checked the identity papers of the five Africans in the Mercedes Benz car but not those of the only Caucasian who was with us. This omission occupied us in discussions as to whether it was a simple human error by a tired official or whether it was an indication of the racial profiling characteristic of the World System that treated individuals perceived to be peripheral with more suspicion than individuals perceived to be core. For all you know, the white guy could have been a rebel from Albania or Chechnya sneaking into the US while some of the Africans quizzed were actually American citizens.

The application of WST to global terrorism raises difficult questions for conventional criminology. This is the type of question raised in my book that launched this series, *Black Women and the Criminal Justice System.* The question is that since it is true that States also commit crimes against individuals and against other States, how come criminologists have no theory of structural penology for dealing with the criminal State? Dr Onwudiwe renews this challenge indirectly here by reminding criminologists that terrorism is not a crime that is committed only by individuals against the State but one that is more dangerous when sponsored by a State against its citizens or against another State. This is close to the challenge of Schwendinger and Schwendinger in the 1970s that the definition of crime should be expanded to include human rights violations – a challenge that was almost completely ignored until the 1990s when Stan Cohen started challenging the conspiracy of silence by criminologists on what the Nigerian human rights attorney, Gani Fawehinmi calls 'executive lawlessness' or what the South African Justice Minister, Dullah Omar, calls 'crimes of the state.'

The novelty offered by Dr Onwudiwe is that even when there is no specific human rights violation, the development of underdevelopment by imperialism should be seen as a major cause of acts of terrorism. This is true in the sense that avoidable poverty in the midst of plenty within the global village is in every sense as violent, if not more violent, than some acts of terrorism that might be provoked at the individual or State level by perceived social injustice and dictatorial suppression of legitimate protest, respectively.

The policy efficacy of this theoretical insight comes from the indirect suggestion in the book that the global community should be more sceptical of the racial profiling type of conclusion from the RAND report on terrorism that core States are more frequently the targets of terrorism by émigré groups. On the contrary, many acts of terrorism in the core States and semi-peripheral or peripheral States happen to be domestic rather than being imported from the periphery. The suggestion here is that all States in the world system should recognise how anti-poor policies make them complicit in the crime of terrorism. The penology for the terrorist state, according to the logic of this book, cannot be the conventional penology of incarceration or incapacitation – you cannot jail or electrocute the terrorist State.

The structural penology implicit in this book will go along the lines of restorative justice. For example, if a fraction of the trillions of dollars spent globally on the war against terrorism was spent fighting poverty and inequality in support of the struggle for deepening democracy in civil societies, there would be less social injustice and therefore, less terrorism of any kind.

Dr Biko Agozino
Associate Professor
Indiana University of Pennsylvania

Preface

This book is the brainchild of my dissertation (all errors and mistakes are mine) submitted to the School of Criminology at Florida State University in 1993. I have endeavored to review it and add unsullied new ideas and a fresh chapter aiming at capturing the global nature of terrorism today in a delicate new millennium. The proliferation of the weapons of mass obliteration makes the new century a dangerous world. Nefarious terrorists may resort to the use of slack weapons for ideological boost up for their divergent causes. This book principally argued that terrorism may be a result of global inequality and gluttony as demonstrated in the history of colonialism and neo-colonialism between the rich and poor nations. Colonialism and neo-colonialism have been blamed for lack of economic development and economic dependency of the poorer nations of the world. The critical point addressed is that unequal economic, political, and military relationships exist between core, semiperiphery, and periphery countries, which may lead to some patterns of terrorism in the world system.

Chapter one of this book stressed the need to use WST to study the effects of international relationships on international and national patterns of terrorism by placing emphasis on the link between terrorism and WST. Chapter one was primarily focused to a review of WST. Readers are acquainted with the meaning and value of this theory to comparative studies in criminology and terrorism. Basically, WST argues that the pattern of a nation's development depends on the nation's position in the world economy (Wallerstein, 1979). In WST, there are chiefly three components of the WS: core, periphery, and semiperiphery. The core is made up of the most powerful countries such as U.S., Great Britain, and Germany. Semiperipheral nations maintain the equilibrium between the core and the periphery. These include nations like Spain, Iran, and Israel. Peripheral nations are the most exploited and least powerful nations in the world. These consist of countries like Mali, Peru, and Lebanon.

In chapter one, emphasis was placed on classification of countries in the world economic order; global inequality and WST; the development of underdevelopment; and criticisms of WST. The chapter concluded by arguing that WST is an indispensable tool to be employed in order to understand the changing blueprint of the international community as it exists today. No country is solely independent which makes it important to adopt WST to help explain the extent of global inequalities and its positive impact on the resurgence of terrorism in the world.

Chapter two examined the definition of terrorism and its different parts. Since the definition of what constitutes terrorism is in the eyes of the beholder or who is doing the defining, several definitions of terrorism as found in the literature were provided. Attempt was also made in chapter two not to rely on the one sided definition of terrorism as violent behavior targeted against the legitimacy of the state.

In this chapter the preferred definition of terrorism was based on the distinction between common and state terrorism. As stated in chapter two, common terrorism is violent behavior directed against states or governments, while state terrorism constitutes violent or economic terror employed by states against other states (Lynch and Groves, 1989; Herman, 1983). Chapter two maintained that state sponsored terrorism is the most dangerous type of terrorism. The chapter concluded that regardless of the definition of terrorism, terrorist acts of violence must be condemned especially those that indiscriminately murder innocent citizens. Chapter two concluded by adopting the definition of terrorism as violent acts directed against sovereign states since WST argues that the labeling of terrorism reflects power differentials.

In Chapter three, a structural theory of terrorism was developed. The theory was fundamentally based on the structures of colonialism, imperialism, and neocolonialism employing in toto, Fanon's theory of violence. The argument presented was that structural terrorism/violence occurs in the WS as a result of economic oppression, political repression, external intervention, and the unequal distribution of resources between different classes in different nations. It is these structural forms of colonialism that leads to and directs structural terrorism.

However, it was argued that West African countries have shunned international terrorism due to certain traditional conditions unique in their own cultures. Chapters four and five, explored the methods that will be used to assess the impact of WST on international and national relationships. Emphasis was placed on the measurement of WS position of a nation and the distribution of terrorism and the measurement of terrorism as found in the literature. Snyder and Kick's (1979) classifications with amendments were employed to place countries in different regions of the world. The RAND Chronology of International Terrorism was used as the database to measure terrorism. Chapter six used case studies of three countries to illustrate the labeling of terrorism in the WS.

Through the analysis of tables, it is suggested that more international terrorist events are targeted against the core nations than peripheral or semiperipheral societies. Even when a Semiperipheral nation (e.g., Israel) is targeted, it has a close relationship with a patron state (e.g., U.S.A.). In fact, the U.S.A. was targeted a total of 121 times followed by Israel which experienced 35 incidents. In short, most émigré groups commit terrorist acts of violence against the U.S. targets and other core interests only to seek publicity and sympathy for their divergent ideological and political goals. Chapter seven explored the fundamental issues confronting superterrorism. It treats global terrorism as glocal terrorism, underscoring the hard reality that terrorism is villagized. The proliferation of the technology of war makes terrorism easy to shift from one society to another as a nefarious form of global vengeance.

Finally, in chapter eight, the RSA was used to show the actual relationship between terrorism and the WST. It was implied that the RSA did not practice a constitutional democracy as a result it relied on institutional terror to oppress and suppress the spirits of the opposition. The dictatorship in South Africa used terrorist acts of violence to maintain and sustain the rigid principles of apartheid. Since the government sponsored terrorism against the majority population, the Africans in turn used terrorist tactics to achieve liberation in order to establish a democratic system of government. It was argued that the system of global apartheid in South Africa demonstrates the two faces of terrorism in the WS. Regardless of whether terrorism is from above or below it constitutes criminal acts of violence and it must be criminalized.

The limitation of this study lies in its descriptive nature. Future research should be more empirical. Researchers interested in this area should use more than one-year sample for a better prediction and analysis of the link between the WST and terrorism. The role that power differentials play in the WS's knack to define terrorism is important. Future research should focus more on a country's ability to label terrorism. Perhaps, that will help in developing a more global acceptance of a definition of terrorism. As it is today, a universal definition of terrorism is still in limbo. It is about time for criminologists to come out with ideas of their own without placing too much emphasis on statistical precision. Criminology needs to develop a common theory of terrorism and future research on WS and terrorism may make momentous contributions to the discipline of criminology in a global village.

Acknowledgements

I would like to thank Michael Lynch, my friend, colleague, and academic mentor in criminology and for writing the foreword to this book. I also would like to express my appreciation to Biko Agozino for his encouragement. I thank Howard Rebach for reading and commenting on chapter one of this text. Thanks also to my students at the University of Maryland Eastern Shore (UMES), my former students at the University of South Carolina Spartanburg and Barber-Scotia College. These students have listened assiduously to my ideas on terrorism. I thank them all for their endurance, inquiries, and questions and for opening my eyes on some neglected issues.

Thanks, too, to Robert Harleston, Chair of the Criminal Justice Department at UMES for all his help and understanding. My appreciation goes to Emmanuel Onyeozili, Jonathan Odo, Thomas Mosley, Stanley Deviney, Mbye Lamin, Jay Bishop, and Daniel Okunbor, all of whom are my colleagues and friends at UMES. I also would like to extend my thanks to Ms. Shearn Barkley, secretary of the Criminal Justice Department, Theresa Dadson, and Jennifer Carpenter of the Frederick Douglas Library for the help they rendered me during the course of my research. I thank immensely, Wouhib Worku, a student in the Department of Mathematics and Computer Science for making the pages of this book conform to Ashgate standards. My appreciation goes to Craig Terrell of the Residential Resource Center at UMES and Joe Aydelotte of Kinko's in Salisbury, Maryland. I thank Anne Keirby and Mrs. Rosalind Ebdon of Ashgate for giving me the time needed to complete this manuscript.

Finally, I wish to thank all members of my family for their help and encouragement throughout my stay in the United States and all my friends both in Nigeria and the Diaspora. A special thanks to Ebere and Mamle Onwudiwe for reminding me every year to publish this material. I thank my daughter, Nnenna, my wife, Ify, and my nephew, Charles Ejiogu, for being there for me always.

1. World Systems Theory

Introduction

World Systems Theory (WST) states that the pattern of a nation's development depends on the nation's location in the world economy (Wallerstein, 1979). In recent years, world system theorists (Wallerstein, 1979; Chirot, 1977; Galtung, 1971) have tried to locate countries in different universal divisions of labor, and have applied WST to an increasingly diverse number of social, political and economic problems.

WST has been widely utilized in sociology and political science as an appropriate means for analyzing both international and national problems and relationships. The aim in this section is to apply WST to explain global inequality that in turn, may result in violence, terrorism, and/or crime. WST enriches this book with the possibility of explaining the economic, political, social, and religious relationships among countries. This chapter will cover the following topics:

1. classification of countries in the world economic order;
2. global inequality and WST;
3. the development of underdevelopment;
4. the relevance of WST in comparative study of criminology and terrorism;
5. criticism of WST.

Classifications of Countries in the World Economic Order

WST is a recent theoretical framework developed by Wallerstein in the late 1960s and early 1970s. Wallerstein viewed the world as a system with a single division of labor. He ignored what he called minisystems, an "old world" that had within it a complete division of labor and a single cultural framework. Wallerstein (1974) identified two types of large-scale social systems. The first types are world empires, which emerged from world economies. World empires have a functional division of labor, a strict occupational division of labor, and imperial state control. The second type is world economies. World economies have a multiple political sovereignty with no one domineering imperial state, and a looser "class" division of labor.

According to Wallerstein's (1974) view, China, Egypt and Rome were examples of world empires, within their specific periods in history. Great Britain and France in the nineteenth century are examples of world economies. Wallerstein (1989) argued that world economies are in a better position than world empires to maintain sustained economic development because the market traders have more freedom to engage in market exchange and in the appropriation of surpluses. Such a world economy first emerged in Europe around the sixteenth century and was based on an international differentiated division of labor comprised of three main zones (Wallerstein 1982).

The capitalist world system (WS) emerged during the second half of the fifteenth century when Spain and Portugal engaged in a series of world conquests (Chirot, 1977). West Africa, the Atlantic Islands, the coasts of the Indian Ocean, the Americas, the Philippines and parts of coastal Japan and China were all conquered and linked into a trading network with the western world (Chirot, 1977). The full emergence of the WS in sixteenth century Europe gave rise to the development of market trade. This market economic exchange, known as capitalism, saw the demise of world empires. In Wallerstein's own words "world economies have historically been unstable structures leading either toward disintegration or conquest by one group and hence transformation into a world empire" (Wallerstein, 1974:30).

The modern world is a WS, divided into three tiers as characterized by Chirot (1977: 13).

> Core societies: economically diversified ...rich, powerful societies that are relatively independent of outside controls.
> Peripheral societies: economically overspecialized, relatively poor and weak societies that are subject to manipulation or direct control by the core powers.
> Semi-peripheral societies: societies midway between the core and periphery that are trying to industrialize and diversify their economies. They may be industrializing and rising, "deindustrializing" and pulling into the periphery. (This would occur as the core shifts its economic base or joins alliance against certain nations as in the recent case of Iraq, emphasis not in the original).

Location is important, "a country's position determines its political and economic global influence" (Lynch et al. N.D.). Further, "a nation's location in the world system also accounts for the internal policies of that particular nation. Therefore, it is important to understand the international and national effects of world system location" (Lynch et al. N.D.). The characteristics of nations belonging to different system locations are described in the next sections.

The Core

World system theorists, such as Wallerstein (1979), Evans (1979) and Chirot (1977), have argued that core nations such as the United States, Great Britain, and France dominate the world economy through the provision of managerial expertise and technological innovation and ownership of the primary means of production. The core not only controls the primary means of international production; it determines where production will occur, which nations shall receive new technologies, and which nations shall have their raw materials and labor exploited. The domination of core nations by world capitalism leads to the control and exploitation of peripheral and semiperipheral nations. The core nations use available cheap labor and natural resources of peripheral nations to favor their own economic and political goals.

Core nations control international economic, political, and military power and utilize these advantages to control and dominate the universal modes of production. Core nations determine what happens politically, economically, and militarily in peripheral or third world countries (Lynch et al., N.D.; Evans, 1979). Bollen (1983) asserted that the core's alliance with the "elites" of non-core nations prevents rapid economic development that may encourage democracy in peripheral nations. While the core nations favor democratic systems of government in their own nations, their policies sometimes discourage democratic forms of government in peripheral nations.

Chase-Dunn and Rubinson (1977) claimed that the core nations have a well-integrated domestic economy that is characterized by manufacturing, agriculture, and a high level of productivity and specialization. In core nations, the major pattern of labor exploitation is wage labor and ownership of property. Core countries control the world economy and encourage military cooperation with non-core nations since the core countries control global "means of economic production" (Lynch et al. N.D.; Snyder and Kick, 1979). However, military cooperation with each other (core nations) is paramount, as is the case with NATO. Core nations have less economic dependency than non-core segments of the world (Bollen, 1983). Such a characterization is misleading since core nations depend on the raw materials and cheap labor found in peripheral nations. Thus, WST depicts the world economic order as an interdependent system: each segment in the system is closely connected, and no part of the system could stand on its own.

The Periphery

Peripheral nations have dualistic domestic structures (Chase-Dunn and Rubinson, 1977) with "modern" and "traditional" sectors. The modern sector specializes in mines, plantations, and ports; the traditional sector consists of villages, the bush, and tribal reserves that serve as a labor reserve for the modern sector. ChaseDunn and Robinson (1977) argued that, although the modern sector produces export commodities, its infrastructure is foreign-based and fails to trade with other areas of the periphery. The modern sector of the economy is linked with core nations. The result is a domestic economy that is underdeveloped and dependent on materials imported from and exported to core societies (Chas-Dunn and Rubinson, 1977).

Peripheral nations are the weakest. They possess the least economic, military, and political power. These nations are exploited and dominated by core nations who tap their labor and natural resources for profit. Economic dependency is more obvious in peripheral societies (Bollen, 1983; Evans, 1979; Frank, 1972). The powerful core nations exploit cheaper labor, cheaper raw materials, and unregulated investment opportunities in poor areas (Cardoso and Faletto, 1979; Evans, 1979).

Andre Gunder Frank (1969:7) wrote:

> When we examine this metropolis-satellite structure, we find that each of the satellites, including now underdeveloped Spain and Portugal, serves as an instrument to suck capital or economic surplus out of its own satellites and to channel part of this surplus to the world metropolis of which all are satellites. Moreover, each national and local metropolis serves to impose and maintain the metropolistic structure and

exploitative relationship of this system as long as it serves the interests of the metropolis which take advantage of this global, national and local structure to promote their own development and the enrichment of their ruling classes.

Peripheral nations do not have the global military strength to overcome such a relationship. They serve as economic reserves for the powerful nations. The exploitation and domination of peripheral nations foster oppressive domestic rule, as well as domestic and external violence. For instance, core societies established a tariffs system that restricted the transportation of economic goods between nations. Core countries monopolized trade and exchange in peripheral colonies and used coerced labor in mines, plantations, and ports in societies like South Africa, Indo-China, and Malasia. Peripheral states and colonies are weak. Their economies focus on imports from the core rather than encourage domestic production (Frank, 1969). The core bourgeoisie had the military power to conquer peripheral nations and subject colonial populations to a position of slavery so as to produce raw materials for export based on low or non-wage coerced labor (Chirot, 1977; Rubinson, 1977). However, this situation is not stagnant. Spain in 1550 was a core society and has subsequently become a peripheral nation while Japan has moved from periphery to core status over the last century (Chirot, 1977).

The Semiperiphery

Finally, according to Wallerstein (1982), semiperipheral nations make up the third structural component of the WS. Wallerstein (1982:41) argued that:

> The semiperiphery is needed to make a capitalist world economy run smoothly. Both kinds of world system, the world empire with a redistributive economy and the world economy with a capitalist market economy, involve markedly unequal distribution of rewards.

The semiperiphery nations are intermediate because of their internal structures and functional locations in the WS. The semiperiphery societies engage in business with both the core and the periphery segments of the world (Chase-Dunn and Robinson, 1977).

A semiperipheral society's trading practices rely on a domestic class structure of mixed exploitation that is dependent on whether or not the state is "upwardly or downwardly mobile." Downwardly mobile semiperipheral societies are characterized by "large amounts of fixed capital invested in less competitive industry, political constraints on new investments and high and rigid wage levels" (Chase-Dunn and Robinson, 1977: 457). Upwardly mobile semiperipheral nations "have a wage bill that is relatively low compared to levels of productivity and may engage in mercantile protection of domestic activity and political mobilization of economic development by the state" (Chase-Dunn and Rubinson, 1977: 457).

Semiperipheral nations have particular economic and political roles. The core exploits semiperipheral nations' resources while the semiperiphery, in turn, exploits periphery countries. These intermediate nations are both exploited and exploiters. Wallerstein (1982:43) put it in the following manner:

> The existence of the third category means precisely that the upper stratum is not faced with the unified opposition of all the others because the middle stratum is both exploited and exploiter.

Semiperipheral nations have significant ideological roles in the WS. First, core societies need the balance provided by semi-peripheral societies because semiperipheral elites are much more political and nationalistic than peripheral elites. The middle class in semiperiheral societies is not completely under the state structures and is devoted to establishing a traditional or modern domestic economic independence (Chirot, 1977). Second, semiperipheral nations are better organized and aware of their political and economic rights. It is possible for semiperipheral citizens to engage in an outright violent and terroristic conflict against the core. Third, although their governments are exposed to internal disorder, semiperipheral governments participate in the international power game over economic resources and political sovereignty. Since they are taking an active part in the global resources and markets, semiperipheral nations, unlike peripheral societies, serve a very important ideological role in the WS's structure. Perhaps, the Gulf War serves as a good example to demonstrate the interests served by semiperipheral nations. Iraq is generally considered a semiperipheral nation (Snyder and Kick, 1979; Lynch et al. N.D.), while Kuwait is classified as a peripheral nation (Snyder and Kick, 1979; Lynch et al. N.D.). The Gulf War resulted because Iraq (a semiperipheral) acted against the economic, political, military, and ideological interests of the United States, Great Britain, and France (core nations) by conquering Kuwait (peripheral nation). By conquering and occupying Kuwait, Iraq went against the interest of the core. The core, in order to maintain peaceful hegemony among all segments of society, may allow the semiperiphery to exploit the periphery. Iraq, however, overstepped the limits set by the core nations by being overtly greedy in its exploitation of the periphery. The consequence was the bombing of Iraq to demonstrate that the core still determines how much a semiperipheral nation can exploit a peripheral society. The Gulf War supports the WST position that the core nations have military advantages over all the other areas of the globe. This means that both the periphery and semiperiphery are under the domination and control of the economically, militarily, and politically advanced core nations.

Because of this type of situation, it is difficult to have the same degree of democracy that exists in the core and also in the semiperiphery. For a political economy to have "democratic" institutions requires a literate and fairly affluent population with ready access to the opportunity structure. To the extent that a population has limited access to an opportunity structure, they can be controlled. To the extent that core elites collude with peripheral and semiperipheral elites, to maintain control, democratic institutions cannot evolve. Democratic institutions evolve when a large enough segment of a population has sufficient access to the means of political mobilization to obtain power to protect their wealth.

Bollen (1983) suggests that democracy is a rarity outside the core. There is less redistribution of power within semiperipheral nations (Bollen, 1983). The support of elites in the semiperiphery by the core (military, political, economic) inhibits socioeconomic reforms or progress that may lead to a democratic form of government (Bollen, 1983). These countries endeavor to establish a powerful state in order to limit the influence of the core. In the process, the authoritative leaders tend to rule with an iron hand. Draconian types of laws are needed to contain the dominance of the core and also contain internal dissensions (Chirot, 1977; Bollen, 1983).

Closing comments on classifying WS position

Snyder and Kick (1979) asserted that there is no one particular guideline for classifying nations according to core, periphery and semiperiphery or for evaluating temporal changes in a country's position. Chirot (1977) contended that it is difficult to place communist countries in different WS segments. The WS labels adopted in this book to designate different nation's positions in the WS are descriptive in nature. According to Bollen (1983) "they indicate an international division of labor in which the core is linked to the periphery (and semiperiphery) in dynamic and exploitative ways."

Finally, Chirot (1977) suggested that nations are interconnected with each other and that no segment of the WS is a "self-sufficient island." In Chirot's (1977) analysis, a country's position in the WS is not stagnant. It experiences rapid changes from time to time. Therefore, the world balance of political, military, and economic power is in a constant state of flux. For example, a core nation may become a semiperipheral nation and a semi-peripheral society may in turn become a peripheral nation and so on. Chirot (1977) identified Japan as a semiperipheral nation, while Snyder and Kick (1983) put Japan in the core category. Clearly in more recent years, Japan has shed its semiperipheral status, and has moved into the core. Table 1 illustrates the different terminologies that have been used to qualify these nations and their locations in the WS. (All tables appear on Appendix).

Having completed a review of WS classifications and describing the meaning of WS locations, the next section will review concepts and theories that are related to WST. This review is useful because many WS concepts emerge from or have been embellished by theorists who support theoretical perspectives that resemble WST.

Table 1 shows four different theories of comparative development and the ways in which each perspective classifies nations. The terms in this table will be used throughout the next section, and readers should familiarize themselves with these concepts before proceeding.

Related Concepts and Theories

WST is based upon the idea that all nations participate in a world economic order and that each nation is dependent upon other nations. This dependency brings with it different degrees of power, inequality, development and underdevelopment.

Structural Dependency and Underdevelopment

To understand WST, it is also necessary to comprehend the theory of dependence or underdevelopment. Dependency theory is used to explain development and also to provide conceptual clarity for development and underdevelopment theories and WST. This material will be employed in later chapters to discuss terrorism. The next sections will review the concept of development and development theory, the concept of dependence, types of dependency, the new dependency model, the relationship between dependency and development, and finally the relationship between dependency and imperialism.

Development

African, Asian and Latin American leaders or scholars tend to emphasize the study of national development to understand their economic and social history that gave rise to third world underdevelopment (Portes, 1976). They refer to development in the following areas: economic transformation, social transformation and cultural transformation. According to Portes, economic transformation in the direction of sustained and rapid increases in the national product and the conquest of "decision centers" in manufacturing, may give a particular country a measure of autonomy for guiding its future growth. Social transformation involves a more egalitarian distribution of income and widespread access of the population to "social goods" such as education, health services, adequate housing, recreational facilities, and participation in political decision making. Finally, cultural transformation is the reaffirmation of national identity and traditions. Cultural transformation involves the emergence, in elites and masses alike, of a new self-image, which dispels feelings of second-rate nationality and external subordination (Portes, 1976:55-56).

Even though such terms are widely used in the development literature, there is no single definition of the concept of development. Economic development became a major world issue only after World War II (Gwinn and Goetz, 1990). Many countries became classified as "under developed" marked by low standard of living, low per capita income and stunted economic development after the demise of European colonialism. The designation "underdeveloped" was based on low standards of living in those countries contrasted with higher standards of living in Western

Europe, Canada and the United States (Cwinn and Goetz, 1990). Developing nations are marked by higher standard of living, higher per capita income and increased economic development. They are judged by a per capita income standard and economic development is assumed when a country's per capita income increases (Gwinn and Goetz, 1990).

Some developing countries claimed that colonialism was to blame for perpetuating poverty and the low living standards they experienced. This claim led to economic development programs after independence in these countries prompted by humanitarian objectives to raise the standards of living (Gwinn and Goetz, 1990). Leaders in Latin America, Africa and Asia believed that economic domination by the industrial nations had restricted their desire to develop and they pursued rapid growth and development strategies. Failure to make progress toward development was feared by these leaders since it might mean inability to govern (Gwinn and Goetz, 1990).

However, colonial countries cannot be responsible for all the ills of the developing countries. Many peripheral nations made serious mistakes in domestic and foreign economic policy, which are to blame for poor economic growth. For instance, some nations engaged in protectionist measures that may hamper investment (United Nations, 1988). Also, the borrowing of huge amounts of money from developed nations require that export earnings be used to service external debts (United Nations, 1988). But this is a part of the WS itself. Semiperipheral and peripheral nations needed capital from the core to industrialize their economies and the loans they obtained reinforced the semiperiphery and periphery's dependency on the core.

What is Dependence?

According to dos Santos (1970:143):

> By dependence we mean a situation in which the economy of certain countries is conditioned by the development and expansion of another economy to which the former is subjected. The relation of interdependence between two or more economies, and between these and world trade, assumes the form of dependence when some countries (the dominant ones) can expand and can be self-sustaining, while other countries (the dependent ones) can do this only as a reflection of that expansion, which can have either a positive or a negative effect on their

immediate development.

Dependence or underdevelopment helps to understand the domestic standpoints of peripheral and semiperipheral societies as part of a global economy (dos Santos, 1970). Global market relationships among countries are unequal and take place at the expense of poor countries (Galtung, 1971; dos Santos, 1970; Frank, 1967; Amin, 1976). Reliance on foreign trade has a direct relationship with higher levels of inequality (United Nations Center on Transnational Corporations, 1988; dos Santos, 1970; Linear, 1985). dos Santos (1970:143), claims:

> Trade relations are based on monopolistic control of the market, which leads to the transfer of surplus generated in the dependent countries to the dominant countries. Financial relations are, from the view point of the dominant powers, based on loans and the export of capital, which permit them to receive interest and profits, thus increasing their domestic surplus and strengthening their control over the economies of the other countries.

In order to offset this type of market inequality or violent economic exploitation, some nations may engage in terrorism to publicize these situations. Due to this type of economic disadvantage, dos Santos (1970) argued that some nations might engage in "super" exploitation of manpower domestically, which may cause internal dissension. The effect of core exploitation on dependent nations curtails the development of the dependent nation's domestic markets, reduces technical and cultural ability, and adversely offsets the values and physical health of the masses (dos Santos, 1970; Cardoso, 1972; Evans, 1972).

Types of Dependency

There are many theories of international dependency. Some describe dependence simply as an external reliance. Other theories refer to the process by which peripheral and semiperipheral nations are merged into an international economy characterized by international global inequalities (Chilcote, 1980). Below are forms of development as presented by dependency theorists.

The Development of Under-Development

In "The Development of Underdevelopment" Andre Gunder Frank (1966) argued that core countries and regional metropolises to exploit and appropriate the economy of less developed countries utilized commercial monopoly. In his view, global capitalism developed the metropolis and underdeveloped the periphery. Latin America, according to Frank (1966) and other dependency theorists, is underdeveloped because it has supported the development of more advanced countries "The now developed countries were never underdeveloped, though they may have been undeveloped." Core development occurred because it "sucked" the economic resources of the periphery resulting in income inequalities and divergent cultures which some authors have falsely labeled "dual societies." According to Frank (1966:6):

> The entire "dual society" thesis is false and that the policy recommendations to which it leads will, if acted upon, serve only to intensify and perpetuate the very conditions of under-development they are supposedly designed to remedy.

The relationship of inequality still exists between the metropolis and the satellites. The metropolis still encourages or maintains dependency through multinational corporations and government involvement in education, banking and manufacturing in peripheral nations. Regardless of whether the metropolis is Great Britain, Germany, or the United States, the economic surplus of the periphery is still extracted and exported to the center. This situation is mostly accomplished when the periphery is at its weakest point in history (Frank, 1966; see LaClau, 1971, for criticisms of Frank's theory).

The New-Dependency

A Brazilian sociologist, Theotonio dos Santos has characterized the new dependency theory in his numerous writings as a "technological industrial dependence." According to dos Santos (1970: 144) different forms of dependence can be identified through historical periods:

> Colonial dependence trade export in nature, in which commercial and financial capital in alliance with the colonialist state dominated the

economic relations of the Europeans and the colonies, by means of a trade monopoly complemented by a colonial monopoly of lands, mines, and manpower (serve or slave) in the colonized countries.

Financial dependency consolidated itself at the end of the nineteenth century. It was characterized by domination of capital in hegemonic centers and capital investment in the periphery areas for the development of raw materials to be consumed by the core. A new type of industrial dependency based on multinational investment by corporations emerged in the post World War 11 period. It is this form of dependency that dos Santos called a "technological industrial dependency" (Chilcote, 1980).

It is this latter concern that is most important in dos Santos analysis. He explained that the new dependency on foreign capital curtails the development of Latin American economies. Industrial and/or technological development is impossible without satellite exports, which will yield foreign currency to purchase imported capital goods. However, exports are also related to indigenous sections of the domestic economy controlled by the oligarchies. In turn, the oligarchies are tied to foreign capital which "signifies the remittance abroad of high profits and political dependence on those interests" (dos Santos, 1970: 147).

It is, therefore, evident, in the Latin American context, that the metropolis in control of the foreign capital also commands and determines the marketing of exported products. This process can be realized regardless of peripheral nations' nationalization policies; imposition of taxes; and exchange restrictions on foreign exports (dos Santos, 1970; Chilcote, 1960). dos Santos (1970: 145) asserted that "industrial development is strongly conditioned by the technological monopoly exercised by imperialist centers." It is not surprising that less developed nations are dependent on the importation of technology from advanced developed countries for the development of peripheral nations' industries. But the technology imported from abroad to develop the home industry is not easily obtainable. It belongs to multinational corporations who retain control over the most important sectors of the peripheral nations economy generating a high volume of profit.

This unequal trade relationship leads to trade deficits in the dependent nation, which may result in super exploitation and more dependence on the metropolis. Such inequality limits the growth of the internal market. In dependent nations such as Nigeria and Ghana, super-exploitation by the core translates into "sharp political and military confrontations and social radicalization in these troubled nations" (dos

Santos, 1970). It may also encourage anarchy, fascism, and dictatorship, which may create the opportunity for socialism in these nations (dos Santos, 1970). Finally, as shall be argued later, dependency may encourage terrorist acts of violence.

Dependency and Development

It was Cardoso (1973) who initiated the idea that capitalist development takes place within dependent situations. Although his work was influenced by Lenin's assumptions on imperialism, Cardoso argued that modern capitalism and imperialism differed from Lenin's original conceptions. In Cardoso's view, capital accumulation results from corporate domination rather than financial control as Lenin had argued. Cardoso maintained, "The present trend of imperialist investment allows some degree of local participation in the processor economic production." The old imperialism produced goods (oil, copper, coffee, manganese, etc.) in the dependent economies to be sold and consumed in the advanced developed nations, while the new imperialism engages in shared interests with dependent societies.

Cardoso's notion is that today's multinational corporation's investment in Latin America, for example, is shifting away from raw materials and agriculture to industry. Cardoso cites General Motors, Volkswagen, General Electric and Sears and Roebuck as examples of such corporations. He argued that monopoly capitalism and development are not contradictory since these corporations consist of local and state capital, private national capital, and monopoly international investment. But he contended still that the main goal of these corporations is to extract profit from the dependent local economies. Cardoso recognized the fact that Latin American involvement in international trade and investment is decreasing. He argued that the growth of capitalism is still dependent on peripheral economic exploitation. Finally, Cardoso hypothesized that dependent economies during the period of core monopolistic growth are exporting capital to metropolis economies. Development, in Cardoso's view, is oriented to a reserved, upper class type of market and society.

Cardoso's (1973:115-116) argument led him to criticize other dependency theorists, such as Frank, for the following:

1. Analysis which is based on the naive assumption that imperialism unifies the interests and reactions of dominated nations is a clear oversimplification of

what is really occurring. It does not take into consideration the internal fragmentation of these countries and the attraction that development exerts in different social strata and not only on the upper classes.

2. The term "development of underdevelopment" (in Andre Gunder Frank) summarizes another mistake. In fact, the assumption of a structural "lack of dynamism" in dependent economies because of imperialism misinterprets the actual forms of economic imperialism and presents an imprecise political understanding of the situation. It is necessary to understand that in specific situations it is possible to expect development and dependency.

Cardoso argued that this structural situation couldn't be generalized to all third world societies. They only take place when multinational corporations realize the need for international division of labor and include sectors of the local economy in their goal or strategy of productive investment. Industrial investment or decision making, even if it is owned by the periphery, is still located within the core country.

Lenin's ideas that were similar to Hobson (1938) strongly influenced Cardoso's work. Hobson (1938) argued that the expansion of the multinational corporations might allow international capital to have greater control over third world economies. However, Hobson also posited that no nation, which kept good records and took into account the interest of the majority, would adopt imperialism as a way to maintain its colonial empire. Both Lenin (1966) and Baran (1968) saw imperialism as a political and economic phenomenon. Baran (1968:197) argued that instead of "expanding and deepening the further development of capitalism, all over the universe, the main task of imperialism was to slow down and to control the economic development of underdeveloped countries." Lenin (1966) agreed with Hobson (1938) that imperialism should develop the economy of the periphery but that "finance capital does not want liberty, it wants domination." Finally, Frank (1979) noted that the internalization of world capital makes imperialism an important part of the local market as well as the external one. But he noted that this situation gives foreign firms more power to control what transpires within the peripheral domestic economy. Evans (1979) also argued that even though the internalization of foreign capital gives more power to the owners of the local market, both the multinational and the peripheral state are dependent on each other.

Dependency and Imperialism

As discussed, Hobson, Lenin, Baran, and Cardoso found a relationship between imperialism and dependency.   From Hobson's (1938) perspective, imperialism was seen as a combination of economic expansion and political domination. Evans (1979:16) defined imperialism as "a system of capital accumulation based on the export of capital from advanced countries to less developed regions accompanied by the utilization of political and military resources to protect and maintain the means of production over which control has been acquired."   Cohen (1973:10) defined imperialism as "any relationship of effective domination or control, political or economic, direct or indirect, of one nation over another...." Dominance and dependence among the rich and poor societies characterized this wedlock.

Chilcote (1980) presented three forms of imperialism in historical stages, or what Bergesen (1980) termed cycles of formal colonial rule. According to Chilcote (1980), European mercantilism dominated the old imperialism during the sixteenth and the seventeenth centuries. During the second wave, protectionism increased and core countries adopted neo-mercantile ideas as international markets became more formally structured (Bergesen 1980). During the final period, the cycle was characterized by import restrictions; protectionism and a more regulated core-periphery trade relationship, which gave rise to a new form of imperialism (Chilcote 1980; Bergesen 1980; Fieldhouse, 1961).

Critically, the study of modern imperialism focuses on two different perspectives. Non-Marxists and Marxists have tried to connect or disassociate imperialism and dependency. Some writers emphasize the view from the center and maintain that imperialism is necessary for economic development. Others based their perspective on the periphery arguing that imperialism has a detrimental effect on trade and investment in the less developed economies (Amin 1976; Evans 1979; Frank 1969; dos Santos 1970).

Chilcote (1980) noted that theories of imperialism demonstrated inequality between core and peripheral societies. Some nations have military and economic power, which they use to dominate periphery nations, as well as to perpetuate dependency and exploitation. Non-Marxists address themselves only to political and military explanations, ignoring economic explanations in a global context (Chilcote, 1980).

The experiences of many African nations can be employed to illustrate the consequences of imperialism and dependency. Colonial capitalism, as an imperialist form of dependency economy, was imported throughout Africa during the nineteenth and twentieth centuries. Colonial capitalism failed to do to Africa what it did for Europeans in changing "social relations and liberating the forces of production" (Rodney, 1982). Thus, according to Rodney (1982:27):

> Colonialism was prejudiced against the establishment of industries in Africa, outside of agriculture and the extractive spheres of mining and timber felling. Whenever internal forces seemed to push in the direction of African industrialization, they were deliberately blocked by the colonial governments acting on behalf of the metropolitan industrialists.

Rodney argued that France subsequently abandoned Groundnut oil industries, which were established in Senegal in 1927, because of protests by oil-millers in France. In Nigeria, the Lebanese set up oil mills, which were similarly abdicated. The oil, both in Nigeria and Senegal, was sent to Europe in the form of raw material. Sudanese and Ugandans produced cotton but imported manufactured cotton goods, while Ivory Coast grew cocoa and imported chocolate from Europe. These few examples illustrate the relationship of imperialism and dependency. Although Africans grew the raw materials, they still depended on European colonial masters for finished goods. Colonialism, therefore, discouraged capitalism in Africa rather than encouraged it. It is only recently that African nations (e.g. Nigeria) are embracing the European form of capitalism as a market alternative. The argument above demonstrates that colonial capitalism did not pay African's enough money to maintain themselves and their families. Rather, it created income disparity in the world economic order.

Income Inequality in the World System

Many dependency theorists have argued that underdevelopment increases income inequality among nations (Chase-Dunn, 1975, Evans and Timberlake, 1980; Jackman, 1975). However, it has not been completely accepted among dependency theorists whether economic dependency deters or encourages economic development (Chase-Dunn, 1975; Cardoso and Faletto, 1979; Snyder and Kick, 1979; Jackman, 1982; Bollen, 1977). Galtung (1971) examined core-periphery "trade compositions" and concluded that reliance on exports of primary products was highly related with income inequality. He also found that reliance on trade with a particular core nation exacerbates sectoral income inequality.

Chase-Dunn's (1975) empirical work suggested that foreign capital inflows, coupled with the interests of foreign nationals associated with such financial agreement, inhibit social and economic development. Chase-Dunn's research, which was replicated by Rubinson (1976), found that dependence on external investment had a direct relationship with income inequality (see also Bornshier et al., 1979; and Hoyt 1979).

Amin (1974) and dos Santos (1970) asserted that the economic structure of the periphery is presented in such a way as to allow impediments to development. The less developed areas of the world have been forced into the global economy as suppliers of raw materials that are to be zapped by the core countries (Chase-Dunn, 1975). Poor societies usually produce specific raw material exports, which consist mainly of agriculture or minerals (Chase-Dunn, 1975). However, it was Frank (1969) who first argued that physical peripheral infrastructures developed by imperialism are not designed to serve the interests of the periphery peoples. Frank noted that roads and railroads, among others, are oriented to export raw materials out of the periphery areas by transporting finished goods to core areas of the world. This led a number of theorists to observe that a peripheral economy, which specializes in producing a single raw material, will not grow like a core economy in which production is differentiated (Galtung, 1971; Prebish, 1950).

Rubinson (1976) and Rubinson and Quinlan (1977) found that income inequality exist more significantly in peripheral societies than in core nations. However, Weede (1980) replicated Rubinson's (1976) study and concluded that position in the WS does not affect a country's economic inequality net of economic development. Similarly, Jackman (1980) disputed the findings of Snyder and Kick (1979) and Chase-Dunn (1975) that peripheral societies have experienced lower rates of economic development than core countries and concluded that no study convincingly suggested a direct association between world economic position and rate of economic development. However, Nolan (1983), in a reanalysis of income and economic growth data utilizing Snyder and Kick's indicator of WS position, maintained that dependency retards a nation's economic development.

The material reviewed above, which relates WS position to economic development and economic inequality, is important to the study of terrorism and to criminology more generally. Several criminologists have related economic inequality with crime, and with violent crime in particular. For example, Blau and Blau (1982) observed that studies have earlier related crime to poverty, but that these studies did not clearly emphasize economic inequality. Blau and Blau (1982) asserted it was only Marxian theories and theories of opportunity that focus attention on inequality. As shall be demonstrated in chapter three, one of the pioneers of Marxian criminology argued that crime is caused by the exploitation and oppression of the haves over the have nots which is the product of capitalism (Bonger, 1916). However, this study by no means follows only Marxian analysis. Both Plato and Aristotle, who were noted social thinkers, recognized the relationship between crime and poverty. But it was Quetelet and Guerry in nineteenth century studies that recognized the "economic factor" in the study of crime. These authors demonstrated the importance of relative deprivation in the study of wealth and poverty (Messner, 1980; Radzinowicz, 1971).

    In short, numerous studies have demonstrated how unequal exchange in different wage structures has affected the relationship between the core, semiperiphery, and the periphery (Emanuel, 1972; Baumgartner, et al. 1975). Others argue that inequality and crime have a positive relationship if only metropolitan areas are studied (Eberts and Schwrian, 1968; Braithwaite, 1979) historical vicissitudes are analyzed (Banziger and Wheeler, 1975) or the whole nations of the world are researched (Messner, 1980). What follows is a discussion of the advantage of using WST in comparative studies of criminology and terrorism.

The Relevance of the World System Theory in Comparative Criminology and Comparative Studies of Terrorism

Immanuel Wallerstein's WS comprises a global economic system and places important emphasis on a "single division of labor and multiple cultural systems" (1974:5). The WS as presented by Wallerstein uses the world as its unit of analysis. Since the world is organized as a single economic system, the WS perspective can serve an important function for criminology and the study of terrorism. It will introduce the need to understand the capitalist system and its mode of production, exploitation of labor power in the WS, global inequalities, and global economic and political, as well as cultural and social transformations.

    Chirot (1977) argued that the WS has experienced changes in the twentieth century but that a nation's position in the system can still be strongly associated with that nation's level of development and its domestic political and class division. American criminologists of the past have studied crime only within the American environment until the 1970s (Clinard and Abott 1973; Shelly, 1985) and a modernization perspective dominated most of the studies (Neuman and Berger, 198a; Huggins, 1985). Other perspectives of social change include the WST (Wallerstein, 1979b; Chirot, 1977), interstate dependence perspective (Bach, 1980) and the ecological opportunity perspective (Kick and Lafree, 1985; Neuman and Berger, 1988). Below the differences or assumptions of the dominant perspectives in this area, modernization theory and the WS perspective, are examined.

Modernization Perspective

Modernization can be described as a process in which social and cultural changes follow economic development (Inkeles, 1975). A society moves from being a traditional, undeveloped nation to becoming an economically developed society as it modernizes (Inkeles, 1975). Inkeles (1975) argued that "no one is born modern." Individuals become modern in society based on their different life experiences. Some ethnic groups who have generated individuals who are able to adapt to the realities of a modern world include Swiss Protestants, East European Jews, the Parsis in India, and the Ibo in Nigeria (Inkeles, 1975).

Crime and Modernization Perspective

Modernization theory emphasizes normative forms of behavior, belief systems and modern values. As a result theorists of this persuasion argue that crime is caused by a breakdown of norms and values. According to Neuman and Berger (1988:282):

> The transition from traditional to modern society creates a temporary disequilibrium when modern values and norms come into contact with and disrupt order, cultural patterns, weakening informal social controls and traditional normative-restraints on criminal impulses. Unless new social controls and norms develop, modern individualism and the social conflict associated with growing cultural heterogeneity increase crime.

The modernization perspective also stresses that riots, rebellions and strikes possess identical antecedents (Eisenstadt, 1966). Group behavior (terrorism, crime) may result when a particular nation state is not developing contemporaneously with the rate of rapid modernization or when relative deprivation is experienced by "people who sense a large gap between what they get and what they observe" (Neuman and Berger, 1983; Tilly, 1978). Finally, modernization perspectives tend to view modernization itself as the primary cause of crime.

In short, modernization theory on social change tends to examine cross-national crime rates by focusing on industrialization, social disorganization, urbanization, anomie and modern values in synthesis with the Durkheimian theory of society (Neuman and Berger, 1988). Modernization theory assumes that the nation state or society is the unit of analysis (Bach, 1980; Lynch et al., N.D.; Neuman and Berger, 1988) and that all nations pass through the same stages of development.

Skocpol argues against modernization theory for the following reasons: (a) the tendency to reify the nation state as the sole unit of analysis; (b) the assumption that all countries follow a similar path of growth; (c) the disregard of transnational structures, and, (d) the method of explanation based on a historical ideal types (see skocpol, 1977: 1075 for further discussion). Given these criticisms, a search for a new means of explaining cross-national variation is needed. Such a perspective is readily available in WST.

World System Perspective

A WS perspective assumes that individual nations or states are constituents or fragments of an international global economy (Cardoso, 1977). A WS comprises a "set of singular processes" (Hopkins, 1979) and uses the WS as its unit of analysis (Wallerstein, 1980; Bach, 1980; Timberlake, 1985; Smith, 1984; Lynch et al., N.D.). Thus, according to Hopkins and Wallerstein (1977: 123):

> If there is one thing which distinguishes a world system perspective from any other, it is its insistence that the unit of analysis is a world system defined in terms of juridical, political, cultural, geological... criteria.

Unlike the modernization perspective, WST is not ahistorical. It explains international socioeconomic change based on historical events (e.g. capitalism and its mode of production, and social relations; Lynch et al., N.D.; Wallerstein, 1980; Bach, 1980). WST helps to understand the global inequalities that exist across all nations. WST assumes that international economic inequality creates a WS that is characterized by core, periphery and semiperiphery (Neuman and Berger, 1988). Wallerstein (1976:345), provided the fundamental distinctions between the modernization and the WS perspectives:

> The key difference between a developmentalist and a world-system perspective is in the point of departure, the unit of analysis.   A developmentalist perspective assumes that the unit within which social action principally occurs is a politico-cultural unit - the state, or nation, or people - and seeks to explain differences between these units, including why their economies are different.   A world system perspective assumes, by contrast, that social action takes place in an entity within which there is an ongoing division of labor, and seeks to discover empirically whether such an entity is or is not unified politically or culturally asking theoretically what are the consequences of the existence or nonexistence of such unity.

But how crime and terrorism are distributed in the world is the subject of the next subsection followed by criticism of the WST.

Crime, Terrorism and the World System Perspective

The WS perspective utilizes international economic inequality and social classes as its primary ingredients in the explanation of crime (Neuman and Berger, 1988).   According to Lynch et al. (N.D.), "the most important determinant of crime in WST is world system position." The location of a nation-state in the WS determines its economic conditions, class structure, political institutions, and social relations that have relationship with crime (Neuman and Berger, 1988; Walton, 1982).   Through the use of technology, the colonists or the core countries destroyed the aspirations of the indigenous agriculturists in the periphery, thereby creating surplus populations (Lynch and Groves, 1989) of people with no jobs.   Thus, according to Lynch et al. (N.D.), the WS establishes differential motivations and opportunities for crime, which vary by a nation's location in the WS.

WST can also help to understand how law is used in the WS in order to maintain global economic inequalities and to define crime in a particular way. In South Africa, law was used to oppress the majority population and prevent it from having a democratically elected leader. Colonial law also allowed the colonial masters to create new inequalities by making it possible to expropriate a weak nation's wealth for investment in a strong foreign society. Colonial law was favored over traditional ways of settling disputes and a total abandonment of "self-help criminal justice in the periphery" (Black, 1983). A WS perspective conceptualizes violations of human rights as a form of crime (Lynch and Groves, 1989), which may also, as other types of crimes, be legislated by the state as violations of criminal law.

With these observations in mind, and speaking directly to variations in crime across nations, Lynch et al. (N.D.: 18) expect (a) "core countries to exhibit higher rates of property crime and (b) peripheral countries to exhibit higher rates of violent crime." Core societies are more likely to use sophisticated technology to boost their economic success, thereby creating the opportunity for relative deprivation, which may lead, to a state of anomie. Political instability, military regimes, and economic dependency characterize peripheral nations. Terrorism occurs more in the periphery because the regimes tend to use force to suppress their citizens and the citizens, in return, may use violent means against their regime (Bollen, 1983, Evans 1979, Timberlake and Williams 1984; Fanon, 1963; Newman and Lynch, 1987; Lynch et al., N.D.). Chapter 3 deals more with this particular issue in the effort to connect WST and terrorism.

It should be clear at this point that WST offers a unique means of conceptualizing world and national relations. This position has recently been developed to explain variations in cross-national rates of crime. However, WST has not been applied directly to the study of terrorism. One goal of this book is to demonstrate that a WS perspective can also be utilized in criminology to understand international terrorism networks. For instance, protests, riots, strikes, and political organizing constitute crimes of rebellion, revolution, or resistance that are often looked upon as political actions which a regime may label illegal acts of violence (Neuman and Berger, 1988). Peripheral nations experience more economic scarcity than the core areas in the world. Poor nations, as discussed earlier, are more likely to be exploited, malnourished and perpetually poor. The periphery's dependency on the core may translate into anger against core nations that may result in terrorist acts of violence. Individuals who live in impoverished conditions in peripheral areas "perceive that they are exploited and that they can end this form of exploitation through violence" (Lynch et al. N.D.: 20).

The WS perspective could help criminologists understand inequality and social class in the international world order (Walton, 1982), law, crime rates and criminal behavior (Alford and Friedland, 1985; Lynch and Groves, 1989); collective political behavior and crime (Neuman and Berger, 1988; O'Malley, 1980); crimes of interpersonal violence (Harmer and Stankc, 1985) and terrorist crimes of rebellion (Fannon, 1968; O'Mally, 1980). A more complete discussion of how such a view is constructed and applied will be the focus of Chapter 5. Before this view is set forth, it will be necessary to review some of the criticisms of WST.

Criticisms of the World Systems Theory

Immanuel Wallerstein's WST, which has been described at the beginning of this chapter, needs no further reiteration. However, there are consequences of the WS arrangement, which have yet to be fully reviewed. These issues shall be detailed briefly before stating existing criticisms of WST.

First, due to the WS pattern, citizens in the periphery who are not as skilled as citizens of the core nations have a lower standard of living. Second, peripheral nations lack economic development due to core country's exploitation of the satellite state's resources and this domination retards progress in the third world.   Third, advocates of the WST (Wallerstein, 1979; Chase Dunn, 1981) take the position that there is a continuous gap between the core nations and peripheral societies in terms of economic, social, political and cultural relationships, thereby maintaining the differences and separation between the developed and developing states.

Those scholars who have criticized Wallerstein's theory generally disagree with Wallerstein's view on the role of capitalism as an economic process (Skocpol, 1979; Modelski, 1978; Zolberg, 1979; and Dupuy, 1981).   Skocpol (1977:1075), for example, asserted "Immanuel Wallerstein's *The Modern World System* aims to achieve a clean conceptual break with theories of modernization and thus provides a new theoretical paradigm to guide our investigations of the emergence and development of capitalism, industrialism, and national states." Skocpol (1979:22) criticized Wallerstein's followers who "assume that individual nation-states are instruments used by economically dominant groups to pursue world-market oriented development at home and international economic advantages abroad." Skocpol (1979:22) goes further in her critique of Wallerstein's presentation of capitalism. She states:

> But a different perspective is adopted here, one which holds that nation-states are more fundamentally organizations geared to maintain control of home territories and populations and to undertake actual or potential military competition with other states in the international system. The international states system as a transnational structure of military competition was not originally created by capitalism. Throughout modern world history it represents an analytical autonomous level of transnational reality--interdependent in its structure and dynamics with world capitalism, but not reducible to it.

Skocpol (1977) argued that the modern WS, as presented by Wallerstein, is both theoretically and historically misleading. It is crucial for scholars to apprehend "how and why" capitalism came into existence because Wallerstein failed to review the process accurately (Skocpol, 1977). Based on Skocpol's objections and suggestions that follow, other authors accused Wallerstein of economic reductionism. Both Modelski (1978) and Zolberg (1979) preferred the autonomy of the state system approach to Wallerstein's approach. These authors are more concerned with the theoretical utility of viewing political and economic changes as autonomous subsystems, but are, at the same time, misrepresenting Wallerstein's theory (Chase-Dunn, 1981). In his defense of Wallerstein, Chase-Dunn asserted (1981: 3536):

> Wallerstein's work suggests a reconceptualization of the capitalist mode of production itself, such that references to capitalism do not point simply to market oriented strategies for accumulating surplus value... the capitalist mode of production is a system in which groups pursue both political, military, and profitable strategies, and the winners are those who effectively combine the two. Thus the state system, state building, and geopolitics are the political side of the capitalist mode of production. This mode of production is a feature of the whole world-system, not its parts.

But Skocpol (1977) and Dupuy (1981) had different explanations. Skocpol (1977) argued that Wallerstein's theory couldn't explain the patterns of economic development and the patterns of state development. The modern WS failed to explain the role of the absolute monarchies, its brutal use of coercive force, and bureaucratic control of modern European citizens (Skocpol, 1977). Skocpol (1977) maintained that Wallerstein was misguided by trying to equate the powerful core nations and absolute monarchies. Skocpol (1977) argued, "There were more and stronger absolutisms outside the core than in it." In her critique, both Sweden and Prussia after 1650, illustrate that a very strong state can emerge in a peripheral area, whose economy is purely agrarian, and which once revitalized, can become a very powerful economic state (Skocpol, 1977).

Finally, Skocpol (1977) disagreed with Wallerstein's argument that core nations are strong states. She pointed out that 61of the most progressive core societies are those that have attempted to combine a world economy-oriented capitalism with a decentralized state policy. She admits, however, that most core states are stronger than most peripheral states due to their internal bourgeoisie economic processes, and insisted that the state system existed before the coming of capitalism and this accounts for its relative independence. Although Skocpol (1977) asserted that the state system predated capitalism, since medieval states emerged in England and France before capitalism, her argument may account for the emergence of the interstate system since the sixteenth century (Chase-Dunn, 1981).

Zolberg (1979) suggested that the state system maintained its powers which were independent of the capitalist world economy and incorporated its powers into alliances which resulted into political-military disturbances (e.g., France and the Ottoman empire incorporated their powers against the people of Habsburg (Zolberg, 1979). The alliance was instrumental to France's ability to challenge the house of Habsburg and to successfully incorporate the world-economy into an independent state system and shows the inability of international trade to exist outside of the state-system (Zolberg, 1979).

Using France and French Saint Dominique as case studies in the period of the eighteenth century, Dupuy (1981) argued that it was not capitalism that caused the underdevelopment of the Caribbean during this Period. Rather, underdevelopment was the result of imperial domination and exploitation coupled with the products of slavery. Dupuy (1981:884) blamed feudalism rather than capitalist dominated WS for the lack of Caribbean economic development:

> Whatever capitalist relations, which may have developed during that time, were subordinated to and functioned under the terms of the feudal relations of production and forms of surplus appropriation. It follows from this that the transition to capitalism is not an "inevitable" outcome of the appearance of transition to capitalism in feudalism, but

requires a rupture in the class relations between the dominant and subordinated classes, which in the case of France does not occur until after the French revolution, the destruction of the absolutist state and defeat of the aristocracy.

Despite all the criticisms of the WST, the world is constantly changing and such changes have an impact on the international balance of power. WST may help to understand the effects of these changes on separate states that constitute the international community. It is naive to assume that any country is self-sufficient. There is mutual interdependence between all nations of the world and the WST is designed to deal with this complexity.

Conclusion

In this chapter, it has been suggested that WST can help to explain the extent of global inequalities, as it exists in the world today. Studies have demonstrated that global economic dependency may have a direct impact (determined by income inequality and lower standard of living) on the resurgence of terrorism and or political violence (Rubinson and London, 1991). The next chapter will focus on the varieties of definitions of terrorism as found in the literature.

2. Terrorism: Definitional Problems

Introduction

In line with the goals of this book, this chapter examines the term terrorism, noting its various definitions and components. The main objectives are:

1. Demonstrate the wide variety of definitions of terrorism found in the literature;
2. Show how definitions often focus on one aspect of terrorism;
3. Demonstrate the bias in definitions of terrorism as violent behavior directed at undermining the legitimacy of the state; and
4. Arrive at some conclusion as to how terrorism should be defined for the purpose of this enterprise.

Varieties of Terrorism Definitions

Over the years, numerous researchers have pointed out the difficulty associated with defining the term terrorism. Many tend to avoid the problem of defining of terrorism by placing emphasis on so many dictums such as "today's terrorist is tomorrow's freedom fighter," "terrorism to some is heroism to others," "one man's terrorist is another man's freedom fighter," and so on. Poland (1988) stated that these connotations show the difficulty scholars encounter in their effort to provide a global definition of terrorism for research purposes.

Numerous researchers have, however, endeavored to provide a definition of the term terrorism. To provide an idea of the variety of definitions of terrorism, it would be appropriate to briefly note the findings of Schmid (1983) and Poland (1988). Schmid (1983), for example, cited over one hundred definitions of terrorism in the literature from 1936 to 1983. More recently, Poland (1988) identified the most popular definitions as follows (parentheses indicate original source cited by Poland):

1. An organized pattern of violent behavior designed to influence government policy or intimidate the population for the purpose of influencing government policy (Lodge, 1981).

2. Terror: violence committed by groups in order to intimidate a population or government into granting their demands (Webster, 1983).

3. Terror is symbolic action designed to influence political behavior by extranormal means entailing the use or threat of violence (Thornton, 1964).

4. Terrorism may be defined as violent, criminal behavior designed primarily to generate fear in the community, or a substantial segment of it, for political purposes (National Advisory Committee on Criminal Justice Standards and Goals, 1976).

5. Terrorism is the culturally unacceptable use of threat of violence directed toward symbolic targets to influence political behavior either directly through fear, intimidation, or coercion, or indirectly by affecting attitudes, emotions, or opinions (U.S. Air Force Special Operations School, 1985).

6. Terrorism is non-governmental public violence or its threat performed by an individual or small group and aimed at achieving social or political goals that may be sub-national, national, or international (Krieger, 1977).

7. Terrorism is the use of force, violence, or threats of violence to attain political goals through fear, intimidation, or coercion (Friedlander, 1981).

8. In general the word terrorism is used today to define almost all illegal acts of violence committed for political purposes by

clandestine groups (Sobel, 1975).

Many additional elements could be added to the attempt to identify terrorism. Crayton (1983), for instance, defined terrorism as an effort to obtain or keep power or control through intimidation, by generating a fear of destruction in those terrorized. He argued that terrorists usually operate in units, disguise themselves under the banner of a cause, and believe that they cannot achieve their objectives through legal means. In Crayton's opinion, terrorist groups emerge due to problems that emanate from deprivation, which include minority status, prejudice, disenfranchisement, and poverty, as well as exploitation. Because terrorists lack access to an equitable, responsive social or political system, they obtain publicity through the mass media in order to make their point.

Freedman (1983) defined terrorism as the use of violence to create harms indirectly by victimizing a neutral or innocent third party. Gaucher (1968:14) argued that "[t]he goal of terrorism is not to kill or destroy property but to break the spirit of the opposition. A minister is assassinated, his successor takes warning. A policeman is killed, ten others trembled...." Terrorists, in short, use publicity of their willingness to engage in violence to influence their enemies.

The definitions reviewed above have at least two things in common. First, each addresses the element of fear generated by the terrorist. Second, each examines, to some extent, the terrorist's objective. However, in many other respects, these definitions vary widely. Given this variety of definitions, one might wonder why there is no one universal definition of terrorism.

Factors Affecting the Defining of Terrorism

Definitions of terrorism tend to be narrow and limited by the objectives and values of the scholars who create them. Generally, terrorism researchers have not studied terrorism in its own context or as a contextualized problem. Rather, researchers tend to focus on a single dimension of terrorism and isolate terrorism from the social context in which it is created. Further, the dimension of study selected for analysis varies from one study to the next. The study of terrorism is, in other words, divided into numerous sub-concerns, each of which identifies a different problem as the most important. The problem selected colors the way in which terrorism is viewed and described. This section briefly reviews some of the dominant subdivisions within the field of terrorism research. The sub-concerns reviewed here are:

1. The association between morality, emotions and terrorism;
2. The psychological and criminal dimensions of terrorism;
3. The meaning of terrorism to terrorists;
4. The power to define terrorism, and
5. The distinction between terrorism and terror.

Each area defined above adds something to the overall understanding of the term terrorism. However, because each of the identified concerns is limited in scope, each also introduces a bias that affects the way terrorism is defined, particularly when only one approach is employed. These biases will become more evident through the following review.

Terrorism, Morality, and Emotion

The problem with defining terrorism is not limited to simple disagreements over the content of the definition. The difficulty associated with defining terrorism is compounded by the fact that terrorism is an emotive term (Poland, 1988). In other words, its definition is in the eyes of the beholder. For example, the manner in which a nationalist fighting against economic and political oppression is defined, either as a terrorist or as a freedom fighter, differs depending upon who is doing the defining and the interest the definer has in supporting or suppressing the activity. Likewise, an imperialist lord whose interest focuses on maintaining the economic and political status quo would not define attempts at revolution in the same way as the peasants this revolution is designed to liberate. In short, defining terrorism seems to hinge upon notions of right and wrong, as well as interests.

Wardlaw (1989) argued that the problem of defining terrorism involves questions of morality. Different groups, individuals, organizations, and nations have different interpretations of what constitutes terrorism. In the eyes of so many people, the term terrorism includes making a moral judgment, which means that certain acts of terrorism are morally justifiable. Yet, in the minds of other people, no act of terrorism is justifiable (Wardlaw, 1989).

Wardlaw (1989) utilized the Palestine Liberation Organization (PLO) as an example of this moral-definitional problem.   Israeli government officials see the PLO as a purely terrorist organization, which is politically illegitimate and uses morally unacceptable strategies of violence to achieve its goals. On the other hand, Arab allies view the PLO as a political group, which uses legitimate, morally acceptable and justifiable violence not terrorism -- to achieve rightful (moral) political ends.

In an attempt to escape making moral judgments about what is or is not terrorism, Wardlaw (1989:16) provided the following definition:

> Political terrorism is the use, or threat of use, of violence, by an individual or a group, whether acting for or in opposition to established authority, when such action is designed to create extreme anxiety and/or fear-inducing effects in a target group larger than the immediate victims with the purpose of coercing that group into acceding to the political demands of the perpetrators.

Wardlaw's definition, however, fails to solve the moral dilemma. This definition simply shifts attention to judgments about the political or apolitical goals of a group. Making such judgments also would appear to involve making moral judgments. Thus, to some degree, moral judgments or ideology colors how researchers define terrorism. This appears to be an inescapable part of the problem with defining terrorism. Researchers must be aware that their definitions represent biased points of view and should not present their view as objective or neutral.

The Psychological and Criminal Dimensions of Terrorism

Other researchers define and study terrorism by focusing on its psychological impact. These researchers argue that the key to defining terrorism is identifying its psychological impact on victims, as well as the general public. The National Advisory Committee on Criminal Justice Standards and Goals (1976:4), for example, noted in its report of the *Task Force on Disorders and Terrorism,*

> There is a vast area of true terrorist activity that clearly cannot be termed political, notably that ascribed to the present-day operations of organized

crime. This is true terrorism, exhibiting conscious design to create and maintain a high degree of fear for coercive purposes, but the end is individual or collective gain rather than the achievement of a political objective.

Other researchers argue that terrorist acts of violence, such as hostage taking, killing of innocent persons, and bombings are carried out not only by "crazies," but also by "crusaders" and "criminals" (Hacker, 1977:77). Hacker (1977:77) identified "crazies" as individuals who are emotionally perturbed and who kill with no justifiably apparent reason. In his words, such

> Grotesquely irrational, bizarre actions seem to be the result of thought processes so disturbed that, in contrast with other terrorist dictators such as Hitler or Stalin, he would be considered deranged in any conceivable setting.

For Hacker, the criminal terrorist is a person who uses illegitimate means to achieve a stated individualistic gain. The crusader terrorist is an ideologue whose goal is to change the existing status quo. In both cases, terrorism is defined by understanding the objectives of the terrorist themselves.

The Meaning of Terrorism to the Terrorist

Terrorism researchers also investigate the meaning of terrorism to terrorists in order to define terrorism. However, as Rappoport (1978) suggested, the term terrorism is embedded with different abusive connotations so that no terrorist wants to be identified with it. Rather, every terrorist tries to use the term to qualify his detractors. The same process can be seen in the WS. Powerful core nations define terrorism as an act of violence aimed at destroying the sovereignty of a legitimate, friendly government. Calling it a "revolution" or a "war" when non-allied nations are the targets, however, legitimizes the same behavior. Western intellectuals who take this position totally ignore the impact of colonialism, imperialism and global market imbalance on underdeveloped nations.

Revolutions are not born in a day. Rather, they come about gradually because people are fed up with the economic and political inequality caused by international inequality. Consequently, the definition of terrorism is problematic if it fails to include the impact of economic and political exploitation on poor nations, or fails to include economic terrorism. Nationalists in poor nations tend to look at terrorism as a justified response to the exploitation of the economic resources by core nations. In their view, the suppression of individual liberties by the colonial regime of terror constitutes terrorist acts of violence (Perdue, 1989). In effect, powerless nations are fighting against the ability of powerful nations to label them as terrorists or as "outsiders." When terrorists are defined as outsiders (see next subsection), then violence may be legitimately used to retaliate. Various forms of terror, then, become legitimate (i.e., no longer equated with terrorism) when the target can be identified as a terrorist.

Terror Versus Terrorism

For Thornton (1964:74), terrorism is the use of terror as a "symbolic act." The goal is to gain influence over political behavior through the use or threat of violence. To do so,

> The insurgents must break the tie that binds the mass to the incumbents within... Society and they must remove the structural supports that give society its strength--or at least make those supports seem irrelevant, to the critical problems that the mass must face. This process is one of disorientation, the most characteristic use of terror....

It is evident from this definition that the meaning of terrorism depends upon defining the term terror. Thornton (1964) identified two types of terror. "Enforcement terror" is utilized by the authorities (i.e. those who have political power) to end insurgent attempts to gain control of an existing regime. "Agitational terror" refers to terrorist acts of violence by insurgents whose objective is to revolutionize the existing regime and acquire power. This distinction between enforcement and agitational terror shows that both states and insurgent groups can be terrorists. May (1974) makes a similar distinction, employing the terms "regime of terror" and "siege of terror." The "regime of terror" describes terrorism in the service of established order, while "siege of terror" refers to terrorism in the service of revolutionary movements (see also Gregor 1983). Herman (1983), in a similar argument, labels state terrorism "wholesale" terror and terror directed at the state as "retail" terror. In short, governments use terror, while rebels, insurgents, freedom fighters, and revolutionaries use terrorism. Terror constitutes the threat of fear which is manufactured by governmental agents, such as police and the military, and which is spread by a legitimate authority. Terrorism refers to the execution and the spread of fear by revolutionaries.

If governments use terror and terrorism is used by rebels, one of these behaviors, by virtue of its association with a legitimate authority, is viewed as "morally superior," "lawful," and "just." The state's violent behavior is not only seen as legitimate, but as "good." Since the state has the right to use violence and the ability to label violence as unjust, the terrorist is easily labeled as an outsider.

Terrorism: A Label that Defines "Outsiders"

Regardless of the specific way in which researchers define terrorism, we must ultimately realize that the term terrorism becomes a tag of defamation, a means of excluding those so labeled from human standing. When the term terrorism is used to describe the actions of nationalists who use violence against established economic and political structures, it tends to shape the opinions and reactions of others in the world order. Nationalist fighters are automatically reduced to a position of international lepers when the intentions behind their behavior are ignored and terrorism is defined unidimensionally. Thus, in the struggle for equality, the terrorist's objectives, ideology and the historical forces behind terrorism are ignored. Hence the stigmatization of terrorism has itself a terrifying power (Perdue, 1989).

The manner in which terrorism is defined, as should now be clear, depends on who acts and who defines. Thus, power is an essential characteristic in the definitional process of terrorism (Herman 1983). Since it is important to examine international patterns of terrorism, it makes sense to examine the effect of international power relations on the definition of terrorism. One way to address international power differentials is to use a WS perspective, reviewed in chapter one. As you recall, this view depicts the world as a system composed of unequal sectors (the core, semiperiphery and the periphery) and highlights how the nature of world order, its economic, historical and political dimensions impact international and national policies and programs. This approach may make important contributions when applied to the area of terrorism.

This claim will be examined further in chapter five.

The relevance of WST at this point is that it highlights the need to examine world processes like terrorism in the context of world relations, history, economics and politics. It is essential not to ignore historical, economic and political domination of the periphery by the core nations of the world in any construction or analysis of the definition of terrorism. It is important to recognize these factors because the ideological construction of the term terrorism is a function of power. Those who have power label terrorism like criminal behavior. As far as terrorism is concerned, only core nations have the ability to label behaviors as terrorist, to control events, and to impose one's culture upon others against their will. It is neither novel nor unique to argue that powerful nations plunder the human and natural resources of the periphery territories. A definition of terrorism will continue to be problematic unless it recognizes that the destructive effect of colonialism on periphery territories is a form of terrorism.

In short, the argument here is as follows. Traditional definitions of terrorism are one-sided. They focus attention on aspects of terrorism that define powerful nations as legitimate entities and actors (e.g., see literature on the morality of terrorism), while defining the same acts undertaken by powerless nations and individuals as illegitimate (i.e., terrorism). Such tactics focus attention on the "sick" or "crazy" terrorist (e.g., see Hacker, reviewed above), and fail to examine the structural inequalities that help create terrorism. The contemporary world is dominated by a handful of powerful nations. This means that nations or groups attempting to alter world order will be defined as terrorists. It also means that while certain "terrorist" acts will be seen as legitimate, others will be viewed as illegitimate. Thus, to truly understand terrorism on an international scale, one needs to examine world order, world power, and the historical and political factors that reproduce that order and create terrorism, the ability to define terrorism and the ability to escape the terrorism label. Thus, it is only by examining these factors that we can begin to understand why terrorism is defined as it is today. Concepts such as the WS, core membership, colonialization, imperialism, peripheral membership and power are essential to this type of analysis. These elements of world social structure emerged at a particular point in history, meaning that the emergence of terrorism might be linked to historical stages of development. Consequently, to fully appreciate terrorism, it is necessary to understand its connection to history or to treat terrorism in an historical context.

Having reviewed some of the factors and views that make it difficult to construct a precise and non-biased definition of terrorism, the next section will begin to introduce additional materials necessary to understand terrorism in the context of world history and development. This material will be employed more fully in chapter three to construct a WST view of terrorism.

Terrorism and History

Revolutions do not occur in a vacuum. They occur in social structures and historical settings where change is resisted by the powers that be. It was argued earlier, using WST that all nations belong to a structure or world system. But, exactly how does this historically specific structure affect terrorism? The brief answer found in the terrorism literature, which will be expanded upon in chapter three, is as follows. Employing a structural model, Targ (1988) argued that terrorism characterized by violence is more likely to happen in pre-capitalist or early capitalist stages of world development. During these eras, exploited periphery and semiperiphery nations may use violence to destroy the core structures that penetrate non-core areas as a form of protest. Targ (1988) contended that violence, terrorism, and political action are conditioned by social structures such as occupation, ruling class control of the means of production, character and level of exploitation, and the ideological structure of society. This insight can be employed to suggest that the location of a nation within the WS may determine the amount and type of terrorism it experiences or generates -- or that the WS gives rise to what is labeled here as structural terrorism.

Institutional, Political and Structural Terrorism

Thus far, the basic literature that attempts to define terrorism, terror, and various aspects of these behaviors has been reviewed. It has also been articulated that many definitions of terrorism are inadequate because they fail to embrace the concepts of colonialism and imperialism, meaning that the powerful will never be defined as terrorist or as those who employ terror. In short, global power differentials often tend to obscure the reality of institutional terror. Below are brief examples of the types of colonial behaviors that could be interpreted as institutionalized terrorism if the definition of the term terrorism were broadened.

From the sixteenth to the nineteenth century, Africans and a few Native American Indians who were used as slaves and sold built the plantations of the New World into bondage. To some African nationalists such acts constituted terrorism. However, as noted above, most scholarly definitions of terrorism would exclude these acts from consideration. How can these two views be reconciled? Can terrorism be redefined in this book to fit the purpose of this research? Definitions of terrorism have at least two things in common: the generation of fear and political objectives of the terrorist. Terrorists use fear as a tactic to obtain certain political goals. This association gives rise to a related term, political terrorism.

Wardlaw (1989:16) defined political terrorism as:

> The use, or threat of use, of violence by an individual or a group, whether acting for or in opposition to established authority, when such action is designed to create extreme anxiety and/or fear-inducing effects in a target group larger than the immediate victims with the purpose of coercing that group into acceding to the political demands of the perpetrators.

He further asserted that political terrorism is a deliberate means to an end and that terrorism is not mindless but rather has goals. Gurr (1988) took the position that terrorism is a state of mind. Therefore, political terrorism is the state of mind of political actors who are troubled by the fear of sudden attack. Stohl (1984) argued that political terrorism is a "theater" or drama, which uses the universe as its stage. Stohl (1988) maintained that violence; intimidation, fear and death are the essential theatrical ingredients of political terrorism. In contrast, structural terrorism may be defined as the response to economic imbalance caused by imperial exploitation of powerless societies in the WS as a whole. To fully define structural terrorism, knowledge of imperialism, colonialism and the world system is essential. These concepts are reviewed briefly below.

Structural Terrorism in the World System

According to Immanuel Wallerstein (1979), there is a difference between conventional conceptions of empire based on conquest and political tyranny (e.g., Egypt, Rome), and a "modern world system" based on economic exploitation. WS analysis represents nation-states with colonial linkages operating within the framework of a world economy. In this view, the world is composed of three sectors: core, semiperiphery and periphery. Core societies represented the center of the colonial system. Inherent structural forces that impelled them to establish territories in different parts of the world encouraged core societies. These territories represented new sources of raw materials, cheap labor, new markets and outposts for investment capital (Perdue, 1989).

The colonization process set into motion by the structure of the WS transformed indigenous (non-core) economies, established colonial administrations, the forced imposition of western laws and customs, and the education and training of a labor force to fit the needs of the colonial economy (Perdue, 1989). Fanon, in the *Wretched of the Earth* (1982) and *A Dying Colonialism* (1965) captured the essence of imperial terror and structures of terrorism. The official colonial state was directly under the auspices of the metropolis, which had the responsibility of making and enforcing imperial (core) policies through intimidation and fear.

The question of terrorism takes on new meaning when viewed from the perspective of a transnational market system based on an international and hierarchical division of labor. It is within this world economic order that materially powerful actors try to safeguard the imperatives of that system, including world economic growth, the establishment and expansion of developmental organizations, open and secure transnational investments, free enterprise, decreased labor costs, technological solutions and so on. Perdue (1989) argued that put together, these factors lead to a growth, rather than distribution, model of development, which is legitimized and based in the ideology of modernization. All of this favors the core, legitimizing its actions and power, and the system from which its power is drawn.

Perdue (1989) argued, "it is within the human consequences of such a system of global reach that the question of terrorism may be joined." The separation inherent in world market crisis or competition has a relationship to regime terror. Perdue asserted that the great powers are not immune from using institutional terror against human beings. As a result, developing nations are used as a source of cheap labor and resources, and are characterized by debt and unequal exchange. Thus, according to Perdue (1989:42):

[W]hat is modernized is a system of global inequality, and what is developed are the dependency relations of peripheral underdevelopment. This simply put, is real terrorism. It is this transnational system that drives the policies of its dominant states, including the use of military force....

Core nations have a strong political and military defense that enables them to preserve the international and hierarchical division of labor. It has also been argued that the international and domestic practices of the core are patterned for the purpose of governing the satellite societies through intimidation and fear. Following the argument to be made on state terrorism, a more acceptable definition of terrorism will be designed so as to encompass the impact of colonialism and imperialism on periphery and semiperiphery nations.

As WST makes clear, terror is not the sole or most important mechanism for maintaining international economic inequality. Unequal exchange and control of technology and the means of production are the primary means by which inequality is maintained between nations in the WS. However, when these mechanisms break down or when they are challenged, state terrorism may be brought into play.

State Sponsored and Common Terrorism

It has already been stated that powerful nations sometimes use institutional terror to maintain cheap labor and natural resources in third world nations. Poor nations can also use terrorism as a means to express dissatisfaction with developed nations.

Terrorism is a label created by the powerful nations. Lynch and Groves (1989) argued that the utilization of this label is solely within the domain of the state, which has the power to ignore or vilify behavior. The powerful define terrorism in a way that excludes their own behavior, and the behavior of their allies, from scrutiny (Herman, 1987; Lynch and Groves, 1989). Examples of this means of labeling terrorism are provided below.

When the Reagan administration took office, state sponsored terrorism was on its list of foreign policy priorities. The finger was on the USSR. Alexander Haig (Former Secretary of State) claimed that the USSR was the primary sponsor of international terrorism (United States Department of State, 1981). In the past, the U.S. seemed quite willing to apply the label "terrorist" to many non-allied states. The opposite tendency (i.e., not labeling states as terrorists) occurs even when it is clear that U.S. allied nations are engaged in terrorism. Syria provides an example of this point. This case demonstrates that the concept of state sponsored terrorism lacks clarity and consistency. Further, this case illustrates how the states are labeled as terrorists primarily, for political purposes (Wardlaw, 1989).

In 1986 U.S. government authorities asserted that "although Syria's involvement in terrorism may be much more professional, much more deadly" than Libya's, evidence concerning Syria's participation in international terrorism is still unclear (Perdue, 1988). Other powerful core nations, Britain and France, have also been reluctant to name Syria as a terrorist state. In this case, it appears that reluctance to label Syria as a terrorist state was related to U.S., British and French interests in the Middle East. Further, Syria's assistance was needed to negotiate for U.S., British, and French citizens held hostage by different terrorist groups in the Persian Gulf. Syria is also important in the pivotal role it might play in finding peaceful solutions to Middle East Conflicts (Wardlaw, 1989).

The U.S has often named Libya, a U.S. non-allied nation, as a sponsor of state terrorism. There is little doubt that Libya has been involved in many acts of international terrorism (Wardlaw, 1989). It has been alleged that Libyan oil revenues aid effort to sponsor terrorism abroad.

In short, the brief examples noted above illustrate how non-core, U.S. non-allied nations (Libya and the USSR) have been defined as terrorist states. On one hand, core nations label nations that facilitate acts that conflict with their interests as terrorists. On the other hand, core allies, even those, which have been acknowledged to engage in terrorism, are not labeled as terrorists as long as core interests are served.

Evidence from the real world makes it clear that core nations have the power to define non-core states as terrorist states, or that state terrorism is only viewed as behavior engaged in by powerless, non-core states when their behavior interferes with the interests of powerful core nations. Such a view of state and/or political terrorism has rarely been made in the criminological literature.

Such conventional and narrow views of terrorism are rejected. Terrorism is rather viewed from Herman's (1983; see also Lynch and Groves, 1989) distinctions between "common" or "non-state" terrorism and "state" terrorism. According to Lynch and Groves (1989: 40), "common terrorism is violent behavior directed against political authorities (i.e. states or governments), while state terrorism is violent or economic terror used by governments against other governments." Many terrorism experts have tried to distinguish types of terrorism in this manner to emphasize that terrorism can be violence by state officials employed against citizens, as well as violence against government officials (Herman, 1987; Lynch and Groves, 1989; Stohl and Lopez, 1984; Shank, 1987). But whether it is official (state) or non-official (common) terrorism, it has some ideology, purpose or motive.

The Ideology of Terrorism

Ideology is an important area that distinguishes one terrorist group from another and terrorists from non-terrorists (Newman and Lynch, 1987). Very often, however, the ideology of those who define terrorism and terrorists determines who will be seen as the terrorist and which behaviors will be labeled as terrorism. To address this later claim, the political dimension of ideology shall be discussed later in this section. To begin this discussion, however, it is necessary to turn to a definition of the term ideology. The term ideology has many meanings. It is viewed here as consisting of a system of thoughts possessed by certain individuals, or a set of principles espoused by political groups.

Ideology does not emerge in vacuity. It is shaped by structural factors (Miller, 1974; Perdue, 1989; Vetter and Perlstein, 1991). Ideologies have a history. Ideas embody and arise from struggles for power and are characterized by historical events. Thus, according to Perdue (1986), the privileged groups in a divided world who gain more from the hierarchical order of that world often view the world differently than the dispossessed. Those in powerful positions have greater access to institutions such as education, media, and religion that shape beliefs. From a WS view, this means core nations will have the greatest impact on determining beliefs about who is or is not a terrorist.

Mannheim (1968: 55-59) differentiated between two forms of ideology, the "particular" and the "total." Particular ideology asserts that opposing groups share similar views for questioning truth. Total ideology, on the other hand, rejects motivation while concentrating on different intellectual universal thought systems. It focuses on relationships between social forces and worldviews with emphasis on those that favor the status quo and those that favor change. It is this total ideology, which appears to be operating at the level of the WS.

Mannheim (1968) views ideology as universal thought systems held by world ruling class groups whose interest is to keep things the way they are. Mannheim (1968: 40) asserts that:

> Ruling groups can in their thinking become so intensively interest-bound to a situation that they are simply no longer able to see certain facts, which would undermine their sense of domination.

In his analysis of Mannheim's ideological thesis, Perdue (1989: 7-8) made the following observations:

> Utopian thinking for Mannheim represented an opposing constellation. Her total systems of thought are forged by oppressed groups interested in the transformation of social or global orders. From the utopian side the purpose of social thought is not simply to diagnose (much less legitimate) existing reality. It is rather to provide a rationally justifiable system of ideas to legitimate and direct change. Utopian thought thus means that oppressed groups selectively perceive only those elements in the situation, which tend to negate it.

Perdue (1989) asserted that the conflict over ideas about terrorism embrace and alter power relations which may result in social change. National liberation movements' accused of real terrorism may limit the use of violence in order to achieve international recognition. Mannheim's view on total ideology is seen in the following example, which also speaks to the core's use and control of ideology concerning terrorism.

In his address to the American Bar Association, President Reagan argued that there was evidence of what he called "a new international ... murder incorporated." Reagan argued that some are criminals who engage in indiscriminate murder of Americans. Reagan stated his views as follows:

> So, there we have it: Iran, Libya, North Korea, Cuba, Nicaragua--continents away, tens and thousands of miles apart, but the same goals and objectives. I submit to you that the growth in terrorism in recent years results from the increasing involvement of these states in terrorism in every region of the world. Most of the terrorists who are kidnapping and murdering American citizens and attacking American installations are being trained, financed, and directly or indirectly controlled by a core group of radical and totalitarian governments-a new international version of "Murder Incorporated." And all of these states are united by one,

simple criminal phenomenon--their fanatical hatred of the United States, our people, our way of life, our international stature. (From Ronald Reagan, "The New Network of Terrorist States," an address to the American Bar Association, Washington D.C., July 8, 1985).

In fact, when we speak of the ideology of terrorism, we cannot speak solely of the terrorist's own ideology. We must also investigate the ideology of those who label terrorism and terrorists. Using the insights of WST, it can be argued that definitions of terrorism and terrorists will reflect the ideology of those with the power to define: core nations. Consequently, the way in which terrorism is defined has a political-ideological dimension. This notion is reviewed below.

The Political Dimension of Terrorism Ideologies

For decades, Western constructions of terrorism used the term terrorism to devalue the actions of nationalists fighting for national liberation or independence (Perdue, 1989). During the 1960s when virtually all-African nations regained their political independence, many African leaders were described as terrorists by powerful core nations (Hutchinson, 1980). In short, some scholars saw political movements in Africa as manifestations of terrorism or communism rather than nationalism.

Jaffe (1988), for example, reported that leaders of the nationalist movements in Africa were labeled as communist inspired agitators. Kwame Nkurumah, the late president of Ghana, was among many nationalist leaders in Africa who were charged with spreading socialism in West Africa (Jaffe, 1985; Ohaebulam, 1977).

Early European political writers, blinded by a colonial-European concept of race, ignored much African history and centuries of modern civilization to depict Africans as "communists" and "socialists" (Fetter, 1979; Ohaegbulam, 1977). These writers believed that people could be divided into different racial groups and that the civilization built by white races in Europe was superior (Jaffe, 1985). African history was rewritten to fit within an emerging European-colonial ideology that justified conquest of African nations.

The point is that early analyses of Africa were defective in their treatment and definition of African nationalism. In fact, European scholars denied the reality of everything they studied and used Europe and European nationalism as their points of reference. The result is that

Eurocentric writers, including early African scholars, distorted African nationalism, its nature, and meaning (Jaffe, 1985; Fetter, 1979). Examples abound to show that the ideological war on nationalism has been historically linked to terrorism.

In Kenya, the Mau-Mau uprising against the British and the Algerian FLN (Front de Liberation) that opposed French colonialism were both linked to terrorism (Hutchinson, 1978). The Simba forces that fought the Belgian imperial rule in Congo were not immune from the ideological-terrorism linkage (Waggoner, 1980). In recent years, ZANU (Zimbabwe African National Union) and ZAPU (Zimbabwe African People's Union), which together ended minority colonial rule in Zimbabwe, were also labeled terrorists (Danaher, 1984). More importantly, Mandela's African National Congress that opposed the racist apartheid regime in South Africa had also been stigmatized (Danaher, 1984).

The use of the label terrorism to delegitimate groups in periphery nations fighting against colonial rule is not limited to Africa. Other national revolutionary movements in Latin America, Malaysia, and Burma have also been tagged terrorists (Perdue, 1989). Wilkinson (1990) identified three major types of revolutionary terrorism that political ideology commonly links to nationalist liberation movements. These include "classical" anarchism and nihilism, third world revolutionism, and new left ideologies of violence.

Classical Anarchism

Anarchism is a result of revolt against oppression. An anarchist, such as Bakunin, is perceived as one who rebels without a cause and who directs his anger against the state. In his militant summons, Bakunin called for violent revolution connected to terrorism (Parry, 1976). Nihilists, in the words of Parry (1976: 107), are described as "the new breed of young radicals of the latter 1850s and early 1860s who valued or recognized nothing as restraining their morals and behavior." Wilkinson (1990) identified Nechayev as the most noted nihilist whose ideas focused on destruction. The Red Army (Sekigen) of Japan, which engaged in hijacking and kidnappings in the 1970s, serves as another example of those who follow nihilist doctrines. The Japanese Red Army has strong ties with Palestine terrorist organizations and its beliefs are patterned after those adopted by revolutionary socialist-communist, with nihilist undertones (Parry, 1976; Laqueur, 1977).

In short, ideologically the anarchist tradition of assassination is closely associated with terrorism. Anarchists do not believe in any form of government that employs political, economic, and social coercion. They are overwhelmingly antigovernment. Anarchists reject religious and political ideologies since they will force man or woman to obey formalized rules or laws.

Third World Revolutionism

Many social activists have influenced third world revolutions. These include Guevara, Debray, Marighela, and Fanon (Wilkinson, 1990; Parry, 1976). However, the works of Fanon demonstrated in his numerous books, are of significant interest. Fanon's books include *Black Skin, White Masks*; *A Dying Colonialism*; *Toward the African Revolution*; and *The Wretched of the Earth*. These books no doubt influenced third world revolutionaries and even the Black Panthers in America (Parry, 1976). Among the ideas Fanon advocated and championed was terrorism (Wilkinson, 1990). Fanon encouraged his followers in Africa and elsewhere to denounce and abandon colonialism. Fanon recommended the use of violence and believed that violence is psychologically beneficial. His message was adopted by the Black Panthers in America as well as by the FLN in Algeria and other numerous nationalist groups (Parry, 1976).

New Left Ideologies

The final characterization of revolutionary ideology by Wilkinson (1990) is New Left Ideologies of violence. Although Wilkinson (1990) did not give a detailed account of this ideology, the New Left is known in America as the Revolutionary Armed Task Force (RATF) and is made up of guerrilla groups. Membership in these dissident groups includes both black and white fugitives that engage in armed robberies (New York Times, 1981). Perhaps these groups are following Marighella's advice that black criminals in prison combine with white radical students to create a successful revolution (Poland, 1989). Groups that follow this terrorist doctrine include Weather Underground Organization (WUO);

Republic of New Africa (RNA); Black Liberation Army (BLA); May 19 Communist Organization; Revolutionary Armed Task Force (RATF); United Freedom Front (UFF), and Armed Resistant Unit (ARU). In addition to left-wing terrorists that the media often discusses, are right-wing terrorist groups. Indeed, in contrast to popular ideology, perhaps the greatest threat to the United States on the ideological continuum is the ideological right (Poland, 1989).

Right-Wing Terrorist

The ideological right desires to maintain the status quo and to destroy the ideological left. The ultimate goal of the ideological right, however, is to overthrow the U.S. Government, substituting a neo-fascist government that would pay allegiance only to the white race (Poland, 1989; Vetter and Perlstein, 1990). Some of the U.S. terrorist groups representing the ideology of the right-wing extremists are as follows: Arizona Patriots; sheriff's Posse Comitatus (SPC); The Aryan Nations; The Covenant, The Sword and the Arm of the Lord (CSA); The Order or Brude Schweigen; United Klans of America; White Patriot Party; and the Ku Klux Klan (KKK). Regardless of how a group is labeled, it is still "dangerous" to someone, and there may be a disadvantage to labeling terrorism according to ideological-political positions (Smith, 1982).

The Disadvantages of Ideological Labels

Vetter and Perlstein (1990) argued that it is confusing to label groups as "left-wing" and "right-wing" respectively, and that it is even more controversial to designate groups as "radical" or "reactionary." However, these labels help illuminate the ideological positions that serve as the base for these extremist groups. Smith (1982, 137) made the following distinctions between left and right extremist wings:

> For the right, the paramount value is order--an ordered society based on a pervasive and binding morality--nd the paramount danger is disorder--social, moral, and political. For the left, the paramount value is justice--a just society based on a fair and equitable distribution of power, wealth, prestige and privilege--and the paramount evil is injustice.

Finally, Wilkinson (1990: 26) observed that:

> Terrorists are fond of using romantic euphemisms for their murderous crimes. They claim to be revolutionary heroes yet they commit cowardly acts and lack the heroic qualities of humanity, magnanimity. They profess to be revolutionary soldiers yet they attack only by stealth, murder and maim the innocent, and disdain all rules and conventions, of war. They claim to bring liberation when in reality they seek power for themselves. Some claim that their violence ennobles them: history shows that it is totally corrupting and ultimately is turned against the revolutionary society itself. They frequently profess that they administer "revolutionary justice", in truth they make war on all ethics and legality and substitute the whim of their own tyranny....

While most scholars depict the acts terrorists engage in as "crimes," not all-terrorist acts are criminal acts. Even those who are concerned with ideology (see the above quote by Wilkinson) make the mistakes of identifying terrorism with crime. In contrast, Newman and Lynch (1987) and Lynch and Groves (1989) have warned that terrorist acts should not be equated with criminal acts. Terrorism has a unique ideological foundation. This distinction separates the criminal from the terrorist, and criminologists thus need to attend to assessing groups' or individuals' ideological commitment. As Newman and Lynch, (1987:224) observed:

> Law enforcement personnel and politicians often argue that acts of terrorists are nothing more than criminal acts, since the victims, after all, are killed or injured, and it matters little to them whether the terrorists have political or other justifications. This is one method state officials use to depoliticize terrorist acts and 'neutralize' the spread of terrorist ideology.

In short, identifying terrorism with crime is theoretically unjustified. Such a comparison removes terrorist behaviors from an appropriate theoretical and social context and makes it more difficult to understand these behaviors. Terrorism, however, must be criminalized if society tends to combat the behavior of terrorists.

Conclusion

The study of modern terrorism is important even though a universally acceptable definition of ideological and political violence have eluded social scientists. Scholars own ideological and political goals and affiliations often make the creation of one definition of terrorism impossible. Further, researchers tend to study terrorism outside the social, economic and political context in which it is created, examining individual and isolated aspects of terrorism.

It is within the reasoning of this sort that I have embarked on studying the link between terrorism and WS. Core nations through the systems of imperialism, colonialism and neocolonialism have exercised control and domination over colonial countries. The maintenance of control in colonial countries did not occur without the exertion of violence. However, such violence is viewed as legitimate, not as terrorism.

In response to colonial repression, the colonized engage in struggles and revolt characterized by violence against foreign rule. Often, the colonized viewed their acts of violence as part of a national liberation movement meant to save their people from extermination. Colonial oppressors, however, did not regard such violence as beneficial and often labeled nationalist freedom movements as terrorist movements.

From the above it is clear that terrorism can be defined in at least two ways. First, terrorism can be defined as the threat or use of violence to affect the behavior of a foreign government and to achieve political, ideological, economic, cultural, and other strategic objectives in the target state. The aim of this form of terrorism (structural terrorism) is to influence the policy of a foreign or satellite government, or intimidate its population through coercion. Second, terrorism can be defined as the employment of selective forms of violence directed against nations by other nations. Criminologists and other terrorism researchers rarely recognize this form of terrorism.

Therefore, terrorism as used in this book is the use of deliberate violence by states and freedom fighters to achieve their divergent objectives. The first definition is an example of freedom fighters or revolts perpetrated by liberation movements against foreign rule, foreign occupation, and economic terrorism. The Jewish revolt against the British rule in Palestine, the American revolution against England, and the

African National Congress resistance against the apartheid regime in South Africa are examples of freedom fighters' forms of terrorism depending, again, on who is doing the defining. The second definition is an example of state terrorism.

While I believe that the above definitions are necessary, there are difficulties with using such terms to examine terrorism. Since those in power control definitions and recording of terrorism, definitions of the state as terrorist will be omitted from existing databases. Elaboration of the type of data available is reviewed in Chapter Four. Further, since the labeling of terrorism reflects power differentials, those most often labeled, as terrorists will, in official terrorist data, be powerless actors. Given the WS argument, relatively powerless actors are located in the periphery and, to a certain extent, the semiperiphery. Given this, and the fact that core nations control official labeling of terrorist acts, I expect official data on terrorism to do the following:

1. Demonstrate higher incidents of terrorism in peripheral and Semiperipheral nations; and
2. Be more likely to define an act as terroristic when the core is targeted.

In order to assess these possibilities, one has to rely on the traditional definition of terrorism as political violence directed at legitimate authorities. While the production and definition of terrorism is in many ways a product of WS organization, culture and history also play an important role in determining the distribution of terrorism (Zeitlin 1981). Certain cultures, like those in West Africa, have shunned terrorism as an appropriate response to situations of economic exploitation and repression/oppression. In other areas of the world, like the Middle East and Ireland, the antecedents of terrorism are firmly rooted in their history, which generates a terrorist culture that may indeed increase incidents of terrorism outside of WS position (Newman and Lynch 1987).

To further illustrate this possibility, case study materials concerning the use of and avoidance of terrorism in a specific African nation will be reviewed in a separate chapter. Chapter four will explore the methods that will be employed in this work to assess the implications of the theory that shall be offered. This chapter will focus on measuring WS position of a nation and measuring terrorism.

3. Terrorism in the World System

Introduction

The goal of this chapter is to articulate a structural theory of terrorism by first making a theoretical argument connecting terrorism and the WS. Second, criminological theories will be reviewed since any new theory must be examined based on the existing theories in the discipline. Third, an attempt will be made to present a coherent structural theory of terrorism, based on Fanon's structural theory of violence that was developed relative to African colonialism. This discussion focuses on political and economic repression and external intervention as sources of violent revolt. Fourth, the argument turns to the effects of colonialism in Africa and the reasons why West African countries have not participated in international terrorism. Different arguments such as resilience of tradition are presented to buttress the position of this book.

Theoretical Discussion Connecting Terrorism and the World System

Many writers have suggested that economic conditions play a vital role in social conflict. Social violence occurs more frequently in poor countries and is more severe in peripheral societies than in rich and core nations (Tilly, 1975; Rude, 1964). Lipset (1960) and Gurr (1971) attributed these conditions to the struggle for scarce resources. In different international societies, the rich are more economically and politically settled, are more likely to be satisfied, and are more likely to support the existing order than the poor.

In general, the social sciences contain a number of explanations of

ecifically, however, not all social science disciplines
ll-developed explanations of terrorism. In particular,
lanations of terrorism are less developed than
d in other social science disciplines (e.g., political
, criminologists draw upon a few general theories of
hypotheses about terrorism. Usually, the hypotheses
ther relative deprivation or subcultural theories of

As noted in a previous chapter, the theories criminologists tend to employ to explain terrorism do not address several important issues including colonialism, imperialism, and neocolonialism as a system of economic, political, social and cultural domination by the core over the peripheral and semiperipheral societies. In order to theoretically link terrorism to the WS, these fundamental structural issues must be addressed.

The fundamental thesis of this book is a simple one. International terrorism occurs because economic, political, social, and culturally colonized (dominated, controlled) peoples adopt the use of force or armed struggle in an attempt to attain or achieve liberation. Conversely, powerful core societies use state terrorism to maintain their vital economic, political, social, and cultural interests over the dominated or oppressed societies. Terrorism therefore has two faces. One represents societies who are trying to keep their economic resources and maintain independence--the other reflects the interest of powerful societies who want to dominate and control the lives of the subjugated. Each nation (peripheral or semiperipheral) adopts terrorism to achieve liberation through political action.

To describe the above assumption more fully, I draw upon Fanon's works. It is the contention of this study, that in a system of global inequality engendered by colonialism, imperialism, and neocolonialism, both dependency and domination result in terrorism. In sum, both common and state terrorism have a similar cause. Common terrorism emerges as a fight for liberation, a fight against injustice and domination. State terrorism is an attempt not only to subdue the liberators, but also an attempt to extend domination and oppression. But national liberation movements do not just emerge out of thin air. National liberation movements are agents of class and national struggle that evolve within the complex dynamics of the modern WS. In the Republic of South Africa, for example, classes and nations emerged in the crucible of colonial experience (Bulham, 1985). History may help to understand the social forces, which gave rise to resistance movements.

Wallerstein (1979) demonstrated that the capitalist world economy existed in Europe in the 16th century. This WS emphasized the endless drive for capital accumulation, the transfer of surplus from proletarian to bourgeois and from periphery to core, the cyclical pattern of alternating stages of economic expansion and stagnation, and the conquest of the periphery by the core. These forces led to the incorporation of the periphery economy into the world economy. This incorporation may take the form of colonialism, imperialism or neocolonialism and forces the reorganization of production, and political structures within the periphery so as to contribute to the overall division of labor in the WS. Again, in the case of republic of South Africa (RSA), the reorganization of production structures involved the development both of cash crops and of mining operations for export in the world market (Ake, 1978; Bulham, 1985).

It may be posited that it is this reorganization of political structures and production structures that created new nations and new classes of oppressors and oppressed. These nations and classes have detrimental as well as positive benefits for the development of the capitalist world economy. Within the WS, imperialist expansion sought to utilize the low-wage labor-power of newly incorporated periphery territories. To achieve this goal, core colonial powers established a three part geographical division of peripheral areas. The purpose of this division was to use the different zones as an efficient means to provide cheap labor and to export peripheral resources profits to the core. Colonial authorities, through classic divide and rule policies (as in the case of many West African Nations) deliberately zapped the economies of the colonies (Wallerstein, 1979; Bulham, 1985; Gamer, 1983). It is within this framework and against this structural reality and the resultant global inequality that resistance movements are born. Most terrorist acts that occur in oppressed nations are domestic, and target governments in an attempt to elicit the attention of the core nations. The rise of anti-colonial resistance leads to the emergence of national liberation movements (Bulham, 1985).

In order to counter colonial oppression, resistance movements may become international in their attempt to be heard. Some also adopt terrorist tactics and strategies to achieve their political and economic place in the world economic distribution. In return, the powers that hold the key to the world economy may counter terrorism, resulting in the two faces of terrorism in the WS. This is clear in Fanon's emotional and intelligent accounts of the colonial system, where he insisted that it is through violence alone that the masses can be liberated. It is also through violence that the masses can be suppressed.

Relying on Fanon's work, blacks constitute and symbolize the essence of what Fanon (1963) called the "wretched of the earth" in South Africa. Fanon's book was dominated by a fierce and burning hatred of colonial and racial oppression. Violent outbreaks in South Africa have focused international attention on the brutality of the apartheid system. It was European global conquest and the WS that created minority rule in South Africa. Although social oppression has existed throughout human history, the phenomenon of core colonialism was fundamentally a European attempt to expand its power (Magubane, 1987). It becomes essential to use Fanon to postulate a structural theory of terrorism. Fanon's writings fit the situations in South Africa today and can appropriately be used to describe events in the WS as a whole.

Fanon's Theory of Terrorism

Fanon (1963: 117) totally favored violence in his books:

> Violence, alone, violence committed by the people, violence organized and educated by its leaders, make it possible for the masses to understand social truths and gives the key to them.

Fanon insisted on the adoption of violence/terrorism because in his view the colonial system is fundamentally a function of violence. In Fanon's analysis, the relation between the African and the conquered rested on a "great array of bayonets and cannon" (Fanon, 1963: 30). Since the colonizer already uses violence, it is essential in Fanon's view that the colonized resort to their own violence--that of "an armed and open struggle." Indeed, according to Fanon (1963: 65) "the existence of an armed struggle" demonstrates the desire of the subjugated to adopt violence as an option. He insisted that the armed struggle was a very important one, which must be used because violence was unavoidable. In Fanon's view, liberation can only be achieved by force. It can be posited that Fanon was purely an anti-imperialist and an anti-colonialist. Fanon also hated capitalism in all forms, both that of the colonizer and equally that of the local follower. But, however he sees the world, Fanon's theory cannot be dismissed as a theoretical account of the development of terrorism.

It is obvious that a glance at what is going on in the world today reflects many of Fanon's views. In South Africa, the situation speaks for itself. The recent Iraq debacle or confrontation between Kuwait and the West also supports Fanon's expressions. In short, Middle Eastern countries, with the exception of Israel, have in one way or the other blamed imperialism as a cause of their terrorist actions. Iran, for example, still calls the United States an imperialist state and claims that the United States has frozen Iranian assets. Ayaltollah Khomeni is still idolized while the Shah of Iran is far-gone in Iranian minds. In every part of the world, Argentina, Philippines, Peru, Pakistan, etc., there is some kind of hatred against one core nation or another. Oppressed periphery nations still believe that the colonizers owe them. In Fanon's (1963:79-81) words:

> Colonialism and imperialism have not paid their score when they withdrew their flags and their police forces from our territories. For centuries the capitalists have behaved in the underdeveloped world like nothing more than war criminals. Deportations, massacres, forced labor, and slavery have been the main methods used by capitalism to increase its wealth, its gold and diamond reserves, and to establish its power . . . . for in a very concrete way Europe has stuffed herself inordinately with the gold and raw materials of the colonial countries: Latin America, China and Africa. From all these continents, under whose eyes Europe today raises up her tower of opulence there has flowed out for centuries towards that same Europe diamonds and oil, silk and cotton, woods and exotic products. Europe is literally the creation of the third world. The wealth which it smothers is that which was stolen from the under developed countries.

In fact, terrorism in this instance has a direct relationship with the WS. In chapter one, I examined WS literature. From this review, it is evident that many Latin American scholars have expressed the same sentiments as Fanon. As developing nations, third world countries cannot provide most of its citizens with stable personal environment. According to Gammer, third world countries were once developed nations. They became "undeveloped" when their political systems separated from their social systems when European commerce was forcefully introduced.

In chapter five, in the analysis of the RAND Chronology, it will be shown that most colonized countries, whether in Asia, Latin America, Middle East or even sub-Saharan Africa were deeply involved in using terrorism as a mode of political and economic expression. Countries such as Philippines, Pakistan, Peru, Colombia, Chile, Lebanon, Iraq, Turkey,

Ethiopia, Mozambique, Zimbabwe etc., were all involved in perpetrating terrorist incidents against core countries. These countries have all experienced colonialism, imperialism and neocolonialism. It may be postulated that these developing countries use terrorism as the last resort to repudiate the core's economic, military and political dictatorship. Having reviewed some of the basic ideas found in Fanon's theory of violence, we may turn to criminological theories after which an attempt will be made to develop a structural WS view of terrorism.

Criminological Theories of Crime and Applications

WS theory provides an international explanation of terrorism. Such a theoretical linkage between WST and terrorism may help illuminate the patterns and distributions of terrorism in contemporary society. Prior theories of crime and violence have not focused on the structures of colonialism, imperialism, and neocolonialism as presented in this book. Thus such a theory provides a preliminary new idea based on Fanon's theory of violence. However, a structural theory of terrorism must be reviewed in terms of general criminological and theoretical perspective. The goal of this section is to demonstrate how criminologists have historically examined crime. This is important since the relationship between WST and terrorism has not been given due consideration in criminological assessments of the causes of criminality and violence. It is also crucial because terrorism has not been defined in such a way as to incorporate the various actors that engage in this type of vicious crime. As the theory argues, a country's economic position in the WS contributes to the level of terrorism targeted against other nations in the world.

Theories of criminality originated with the studies of Quetelet and Lombroso (Shelley, 1981). Quetelet argued that the important concern of criminology was to explain the origin and distribution of crime in society placing emphasis on social factors as the cause of crime. Both Quetelet and the French scholar Guerry produced studies, which permitted a comparison of the incidence of crime with such social factors as age, sex, poverty, geography, education, race, and economics. From the data presented by the two scholars, it became clear that poverty is the source of much crime. They also noticed similarities in the patterns of crime committed in different societies, and concluded that criminologists should apply scientific methods in their study of criminal behavior (Shelley,

1981).

Lombroso, generally acknowledged as the father of modern criminology, is best known for his biological theory of atavism. The theory stated that criminals are evolutionary throwbacks to earlier stages of primitive life. This part of Lombroso's theory is an attempt to explain deviant behavior at the individual unit of analysis, by reference to the most rudimentary biological determinism. Lombroso focused only on the characteristics of the individual offender and ignored the impact of environmental social factors on crime (Jeffery, 1992; Rennie, 1978; Shelley, 1981).

Gabriel Tarde, an early criminologist, presented a theory of crime as normal learned behavior. Tarde ignored Lombroso's theory that crime was caused by biological abnormality. Instead, he argued that criminals were mostly normal people whose criminal propensities were the result of their surrounding environments where they learn to commit crime as a way of life. Tarde's argument was based on his theory of *Laws of Imitation*. He believed that change in society produces the nature of offender population and that social factors such as the growth of urban areas have a profound effect on patterns of criminality in different societies (Rennie, 1978; Shelley, 1981; Vine, 1972).

But it was Durkheim who gave sociology its raison d'être. He argued those social facts such as crime rates or suicide rates can be studied adequately by examining specific social conditions such as the breakdowns of norms throughout a society. Like Gabriel Tarde, Durkheim also emphasized the impact of larger social developments on criminal behavior. Unlike Lombroso, Durkheim's method was radical and required the theorist to remain at the societal level of analysis for explanations of social phenomena, rather than looking for deterministic psychological and biological factors (Rennie, 1978; Shelley, 1981; Vold and Bernard, 1986). Durkheim viewed crime, not only as a sign of progress, but also as a social necessity (Rennie, 1978; Vold and Bernard, 1986).

In short, Durkheim's theses have been well received in criminology and have influenced the discipline. His study of suicide as a social phenomenon to be explained is important. Durkheim argued that during economic expansion rising expectation "surpass the means at their command," expose people to stress, and result in suicide. He believed that the source of high crime rates in organic society rest in normlessness or anomie caused by the rapid social changes associated with modernization. Therefore, Durkheim attributed the high rate of crimes and other forms of delinquent behavior to the normlessness generated by the industrial revolutions. Durkheim's theory of anomie influenced the development of control, strain, and ecological theories in America (Vold and Bernard, 1986; Cullen, 1983; Rennie, 1978).

Another scholar who influenced criminological knowledge was Karl Marx. Both Marx and Engels believed that crime rates increased rapidly with the industrialization of society. Marx was not a criminologist, his ideas about crime centered on the concept of demoralization (Hirst, 1979). Marx believed that it was important that people in society be productive in life and in work. He argued that the industrialized societies have large numbers of unemployed and underemployed people. He believed that those who are jobless in such a society become demoralized and, therefore, have the proclivity to all forms of crime and vice. Marx used the label Lumpenproletariat to describe this group of people who are unproductive and existing outside of the system of economic production (Lynch and Groves, 1989). Those who owned the means of production, Marx called the bourgeoisie while he labeled wage laborers as the proletariat (Lynch and Groves, 1989).

Marx emphasized the necessity to study a society's economic process:

> The economic structure of a society is the real foundation, on which rise legal and political superstructures and to which correspond definite forms of social consciousness. The mode of production in material life determines the general character of the social, political, and spiritual processes of life. It is not the consciousness of men that determines their existence, but, on the contrary, their social existence determines their consciousness (Marx in Lynch and Groves, 1989:12).

Marx's position is that inherent "superstructural" forces including law, politics, education, and consciousness maintain any economic system. Marx saw society as a product of force, constraint, and domination.

An early Marxist criminologist, Willem Bonger (1916), provided support for the Marxian perspective on crime in his book *Criminality and Economic Conditions*. Bonger began by defining crime as "an act within a group of persons that form a social unit, and whose author is punished by the group." Crime in Bonger's view is an immoral act of a serious character. Bonger described four types of crimes: economic, sexual, political, and vengeance. Economic crimes arise in society as a result of unemployment. Bonger, therefore, echoed Marx's theory by arguing that capitalism is the cause of egoism. He believed that criminal behavior is associated with the strains of life under capitalism (Lynch and Groves, 1989).

Moreover, Bonger believed that capitalists are egocentric, greedy and selfish. Since capitalism encouraged such behavior people pursue their individualistic goals at the detriment of others. He believed that crime is concentrated in the lower classes because the criminal justice system criminalizes the activity of the poor but allows the rich to achieve its greedy goals. In short, there is a legal bias within the criminal justice system that favors only the rich. These views have influenced conflicts and radical theorists in U.S.A. today (see Lynch and Groves, 1989; Vold and Bernard, 1986; Quinney, 1980; Turk, 1977).

From Quetelet to Durkheim, throughout the nineteenth century, criminological thinking and studies focused on the significance of larger social forces and societal evolution on crime rates and patterns of criminality. However, these studies did not adequately develop reasoning on the vital impact of industrialization and urbanization on criminality. American theorists were left to explore the full impact of social modernization on deviant behavior (Shelley, 1981). The English criminologist, Sir Leon Radzinowicz (1962), gave the explanation while criminological theory shifted in the twentieth century from Western European to American hands. The United States, he explained, emerged with the highest degree of wealth and at the same period experienced the greatest increase in crime rates. American criminologists broke with Lombrosian theory conducting serious empirical research and testing new criminological hypotheses. Radzinowicz argued that the American criminologists for these reasons have surpassed their European counterparts in this century and have assumed the theoretical lead in criminological thought.

These theories, which dominated international criminology in the twentieth century until the rise of radical and conflict schools of criminology, include anomie, opportunity theory, differential association, culture conflict, social disorganization, relative deprivation, and delinquency subcultures. They will be summarized below.

According to Merton's (1979) anomie theory, all societies have stated goals for their citizenry. The goals are things worth striving for, and pressure exists to attain these goals. The society designates appropriate means for achieving these culturally valued goals. But as Lynch and Groves pointed out, there is an unequal distribution of the opportunities for attaining these goals, which preclude some members of the society from realizing culturally valued ends. As a consequence, some members of the society follow illegitimate or deviant means in order to attain success within that society that is achievement oriented. In the words of Lynch and Groves (1989:76) "reduced to a formula: Pressures + opportunities = Incentives for criminal behavior." Merton's theory was designed for American society but has been applied to the WS in general as an explanation of criminal behavior.

Richard Cloward and Lloyd Olin (1960) developed differential opportunity theory. The theory views the individual in relation to both the legitimate and the illegitimate opportunity structures of society. They believed that crime is most likely to take place "in the social structure where rewards and opportunities are most scarce." Therefore, persons exposed to scarcity are likely to experience discontent and frustration, a sense of indignation and fatal problems of adjustment, a sense of alienation, and feelings of unjust deprivation that undermine the legitimacy of the social order (Lynch and Groves, 1989: 74). According to Lynch and Groves, Merton drew the same analogy when he argued that what people want and expect leads to "intolerable situation" of "frustration and thwarted aspiration" which subsequently produces "a strain toward innovation." Thus the innovations include anti-social behavior, vice, crime, hostilities, exaggerated anxieties, corruption, the entire catalogue of proscribed behaviors (Merton, 1979) and terrorism.

Selling (1938) proposed in culture conflict theory that normative conflict contributes to criminality. He believed that different cultures have different "conduct norms," that is, rules that people are expected to respect in certain circumstances. These rules may in turn become laws within a certain homogeneous society, which may give rise to overlap and contradiction as the society becomes more complex. Selling believed that in colonization situations, laws of one culture may clash with laws of another cultural group and in such a case, law would no longer represent a consensus of the various members of the society, but would remain the rules or conduct norms of the controlling culture. This theory has not been seriously subjected to empirical test to determine its explanatory validity. However, the oppressed usually adopts the laws and culture of the dominant group (Shelley, 1981). It is useful to the trends in contemporary society due to easy mobility that characterizes the WS today (e.g., migration of workers, transportation of weapons of violence). Other criminologists have developed other versions of the conflict theory. These include Vold's group conflict theory (1958); Quinney's theory of the social reality of crime (1970); Turk's theory of criminalization (1969), and Chambliss and Sedman's analysis of the criminal justice system (1971).

In short, conflict theory takes the position that relative powerlessness is a significant structural factor associated with the evolution of patterns of behavior that powerful actors may define as criminal including terrorist acts of violence. This means that the groups that have less power within a society are most likely to be labeled criminals and be processed by the officials of the criminal justice system. In this regard, it can be concluded, that the powerful group within a society possess lower official crime rates, whereas, the powerless group has higher official crime rates.

Edwin Sutherland formulated the differential association theory. C. Ray Jeffery (1991) described Sutherland as the father of American Criminology. His theory which is culture bound has received American and international acceptance (Shelley, 1981). Sutherland's theory posits that in a situation of differential social organization and normative conflict differences in behavior, including criminal and non-criminal behaviors, emerge because of differential association. Since criminal behavior arises in the same shape as non-criminal behavior then, a learning process may explain both. He believed that through the process of communication within any society, members might learn definitions that are either favorable or unfavorable to violating the law. Thus, if a person associates with a terrorist that individual may become a terrorist. In Sutherland's theory, if a non-terrorist moves from one small group characterized by non-terrorism phenomenon to another group characterized by terrorism, that person may learn the techniques of terrorism behavior and may in turn become a terrorist. The theory holds that criminal behavior is learned through interaction with others. Therefore Libya may train Palestinians in Libyan camps as terrorists since both groups interact together. Sutherland's theses that cultural conflicts or complex organization caused by social and economic trends in the WS generated a pervasive individualism and other factors congenial to criminality lend support to such a claim.

Social organization theory, as developed by Shaw and Mckay (1942) is relevant today to regions outside American society that are experiencing the process of economic development (Shelley, 1981). According to this theory, delinquency has its foundations in the dynamics of a community. The theory assumes that delinquency is the result of a breakdown of institutional and community based controls. Members of the community who reside in such environments are not necessarily themselves; they are disoriented individuals, and they are merely looked upon as responding "naturally" to socially disorganized environmental conditions. The theory also assumed that rapid industrialization, urbanization, and immigration often cause the disorganization of community-based institutions, which is more rampant in urban areas. In the ecological areas with low rate of delinquency, consensus toward law, and general societal values exist. In urban areas with high rates of crime, there are conflicting moral values. These neighborhoods pursue crime as the only available means of survival. Furthermore, community residents recognize crime as a viable avenue of maintaining social and economic status. This means that children in areas without values turn to criminal forms of social control.

Relative deprivation theory is not primarily a theory of crime, but it can be used to explain criminal behavior in an urban environment (Shelley, 1981). Relative deprivation occurs in industrialized societies where the lower class, young males, or ethnic minorities feel economically discriminated (e.g. unemployment). It can also exist in a developing society where new metropolitan residents seek to acquire material possessions that were never made available to them before (Shelley, 1-981). For example, after independence, most African leaders stuffed their pockets with African money leading to unnecessary affluence. Those who have the least in such societies may be angry because the society's distribution of wealth is unjust. Therefore, relative deprivation combines economic inequality with feelings of resentment and injustice among those groups who have the least in such a society (Runciman, 1966; Box, 1987; Stack, 1984). Such feelings of resentment characterized by poverty and inequality may lead to terrorist acts of violence.

The subculture approach to crime is characterized by many theories. The theorists are in disagreements on the nature of the subculture but they share a common view that delinquency is associated to the rise of a subculture, which is a culture within a culture. Albert Cohen, R.A. Cloward, and L.E. Olin, and Walter Miller developed these theories in the 1950s. They all emphasized the structure and causes of gang delinquency. They proposed that a fundamental determinant of lower-class gang delinquency is a structurally imposed obstacle or barrier to success in the society. Since this type of delinquency occurs most often among boys, the subculture theories argued that males in such a subculture maintain their own values that are in conflict with the conventional middle class values. They have a separate, identifiable culture distinct from those of the middle class. The lower class youths try to achieve on their own terms. Where the middle class boys have values such as achievement, the lower class has "focal concerns" that include trouble and toughness. The predominance of these values among the lower class helps to explain their proclivity to criminal behavior and the severity of the crimes they commit, as well as their inability to succeed within the established structure of society.

Although Matza (1968) criticized these theories, Wolfgang and Ferracuti (1981) suggested that the theories might help to explain the origin of the subculture. All the theories put together cannot adequately explain why there is a tremendous increase of terrorism in the world today. It becomes necessary to look elsewhere for an explanation. Such a place is the WST, which will help to trace the origin of terrorism in contemporary society. WST can provide criminologists with the theoretical framework needed to examine the evolution of terrorism for the past two hundred years. It uses the nation-states, location in the WS as its unit of analysis. It can help criminologists to understand the dynamics of terrorism in the world and why societies and groups and individual engage in terrorist acts of violence. Most countries involved in international terrorism have in one way or the other experienced the ugly experience of colonialism. WST may sharpen our criminological knowledge and enhance our intellectual ability to master the complexity of the etiology of terrorism and its appearance in different regions of the globe.

The brief examination of criminological theories of the twentieth century demonstrates a total lack of interest in the study of terrorism by criminologists. This is perplexing since international terrorism poses a security threat to the global society. The global world we live in is interconnected. No country is self-sufficient (recent Russian and American partnership is a very good example). WST, unlike existing criminological models, recognizes these international relationships, as it exists in contemporary society. WST gives criminologists the tool necessary to understand not only capitalist societies but also socialist nations and patterns of terrorism. Knowledge of WST expands criminological understanding of peripheral and semiperipheral societies thereby overcoming the weaknesses created by placing emphasis only on core societies and their patterns of criminality. A complete knowledge of WST is essential to the understanding of global theories of criminality, criminal behavior, and terrorism.

Criminology needs new ideas and perspectives that encourage diversity in the study of crime and terrorism. As this review of criminological theories suggests, criminology offers a monolithic view that typically obstructs its object of study from the context in which it is enmeshed. WST provides an appropriate context in which terrorism may be situated and understood. To further understand this context, the next section is devoted to the work of Fanon, one of the most prolific, and critical analysts of colonialism and oppression.

Towards the Development of a Structural World System Theory of Terrorism: An Initial Attempt

This initial presentation of a structural WST of terrorism is predicted to be controversial since its contents are based on this writer's own knowledge of colonialism and imperialism as an African. It is not at all intended to condemn capitalism. Rather the argument is the rejection of foreign or imported capitalism. Peripheral countries such as those found in Africa must endeavor to develop their own domestic economic system structures that revolve around their own native economies. In order for these peripheral nations to develop an ambitious economic program they must rely on native talents. In other words, they must invest in themselves since investment in native talents is the lifeblood of a nation or the engine that moves a country's economic development. Unless reliance on native talents is encouraged peripheral nations will continue to blame core nations for their (peripheral) economic dependency. The only way to attain development is to decolonize peripheral nations and remove their dependency on core technologies. Furthermore, dependency on foreign colonial finance, transportation, industries, manufacturing, agriculture etc., has given rise to structural terrorism in peripheral nations. This structural terrorism may quickly turn into international terrorism.

Thus eliminating dependency has multiple positive outcomes. Peripheral nations need to develop in order to avert both internally and externally directed terrorism. Structural terrorism may be externally as well as domestically oriented. Externally, structural terrorism is the result of the domination-dependency syndrome, which is an essential quality of imperialism. Internally or domestically, structural terrorism is characterized by imperialism's exploitation of people, which give rise to colonial alienation of the individual in the system of production. In such a colonial process of production, the economic, political, cultural, and social forces may also produce alienation because the colonized no longer can function in a way that is congenial for integral development (Ake, 1978).

Peripheral development constitutes a crucial step to eliminate internal and external terrorism (South Africa is a case in point) since these forms of structural terrorism come from exploitation and fragmentation of the majority through a rigid system that denies the majority the right to existence. The immediate outcome of such a situation includes direct refusal to adhere to the rules and regulations determined by the minority authorities or what earlier were referred to as the legitimate authorities. (An argument will be presented in chapter 6, which shows that these legitimate governments are in fact illegitimate.) The rejection of legitimate authorities may be in the forms of revolts, riots, uprisings, protests, civil wars, external and internal terrorism.

The result of violence designed to eliminate core oppression is ultimately peace. Peace is associated with humanity and a redirection of creative energies (Pepinsky and Quinney, 1991). It means that people will possess higher skills, greater freedom, self-confidence, self-discipline, responsibility, creativity based on native talents, and the material well-being needed to survive in a developed society (Nnoli, 1987). Development here implies the ability of the people to actualize and maintain a socioeconomic and cultural system that would be translated into power for conscious participation in a system designed to build their own future (Asante, 1987) For instance, a social-economic and cultural processes may lead to higher production for societal needs based upon non-exploitative relations. It will also be based on equitable distribution of societal goods in a sound environment. It is only through such a development that security may be maintained in such a society (Ake, 1978; Asante, 1987).

By security is meant protection from structural violence. Security may also mean the security of one state from another or the security of the masses from the minority. Threats to the security of a state when another country engages in exploitation of its economic resources including the forced labor of its people, thereby preventing it from achieving its potential survival is also a violation of peace (Asante, 1987; Ake, 1978; Nnoli, 1987).

Peace, security and development are linked together in the WS's relationships and processes. To achieve peace through development in Africa, for example, is a long-range goal. Fanon studied African colonialism, particularly, Algeria in detail. From Fanon's legion of publications, evidence of structural terrorism may be articulated in the following structures of terrorism (e.g., class, peasants, and working class).

Fanon's Structural Terrorism

Imperialism continues to pose a direct threat to all parts of the world including the disbanded former socialist countries. Yugoslavia, countries in the former Soviet Union, Somalia and numerous others have experienced different kinds of continuous crisis. In fact, imperialism of finance capital is the crucial distributor of structural violence. It does so by maintaining an externally oriented system of economic production, structurally connected to the core countries, which marginalizes peripheral economies (Ake, 1978). This is accomplished by maintaining a minority petty bourgeois ruling class in power through economic, political, and military external aid. The maintenance of the petty bourgeois class in peripheral societies excludes the majority of the citizens from the benefit of liberation. Fanon (1963: 139) presented the argument in the following statement:

> The ranks of decked-out profiteers whose grasping hands scrape up the bank notes from a poverty-stricken country will sooner or later be men of straw in the hands of the army, cleverly handled by foreign experts. In this way the former mother country practices indirect government., both by the bourgeoisie that it upholds and also by the national army led by its experts, an army that pins the people down, immobilizing and terrorizing them.

In Africa, for example, core powers interfere, usually through force or threat of force, in conflicts to support factions loyal to the maintenance of the imperialist structures of exploitation. It is this type of support that intensifies structural violence and encourages terrorist responses by peripheral nations. Even in South Africa, the violent and repressive programs of the minority racist regime find some support from core powers seeking to maintain their own economic interests (see chapter one, six and seven for discussions).

Class Structures of Neocolonialism

Fanon (1963) identified the class structures of neocolonialism, which contributes to oppression and creates the conditions for revolution and terrorism. According to Fanon, the oppressed peasants react with some forms of demonstrations, uprisings and revolts, which are quickly and brutally suppressed. Fanon (1963: 48) believes:

> The peasantry is systematically disregarded for the most part by the propaganda put out by the nationalist parties. And it is clear that in the colonial countries the peasants alone are revolutionary, for they have nothing to lose and everything to gain. The starving peasant, outside the class system, is first among the exploited to discover that only violence pays.

Not only did Fanon argue that the peasants are ready to embark on revolutionary force, he also maintains that in the process of the armed struggle, the peasants are capable of leading a violent revolution. Fanon, however, did not have confidence with the working class. Fanon (1963: 88) recognized that the working class can be politically savvy but cannot be trusted to carry out a successful revolution.

> It cannot be too strongly stressed that in the colonized territories the proletariat is the nucleus of the colonized population which has been most pampered by the colonial regime. The embryonic proletariat of the towns is in a comparatively privileged position. In capitalist countries, the working class has nothing to lose; it is they who, in the long run, have everything to gain. In the colonial countries the working class has everything to lose; in reality it represents that fraction of the colonized nation which is necessary and irreplaceable if the colonial machine is to run smoothly; it includes train conductors, taxi drivers, miners, dockers, interpreters, nurses and so on. It is these elements which constitute also the "bourgeois" fraction of the colonized people.

Fanon's dismissal of working class participation in revolutionary struggles may no longer be true in today's society. But since Fanon ignored the working class, he quickly embraced the Lumpenproletariat as the new urban associates. The Lumpenproletariat becomes an important module of Fanon's structures of terrorism in the WS. According to Fanon (1963: 103):

> In fact the rebellion which began in the country districts, will filter into towns through that fraction of the peasant population which is blocked on the outer fringe of the urban centers, that fraction which has not yet succeeded in finding a bone to gnaw in the colonial system. The men whom the growing population of the country districts and colonial

expropriation have brought to desert their family holdings circle tirelessly around the different towns, hoping that one day or another they will be allowed inside. It is within this mass of humanity, this people of the shantytowns, at the core of the Lumpenproletariat, that the rebellion will find its urban spearhead. For the Lumpenproletariat, that horde of starving men, uprooted from their tribe and from their clan, constitutes one of the most spontaneous and the most radically revolutionary forces of a colonized people.

Fanon (1963: 104) believed that the Lumpenproletariat were an essential force for a fruitful revolution:

> So the pimps, the hooligans, the unemployed and the petty criminals, urged on from behind, through themselves into the struggle for liberation like stout working men. These classes idlers will by militant and decisive action discover the path that leads to nationhood.... The prostitutes, too, and the maids who are paid pounds a month, all the hopeless dregs of humanity, all who turn in circles between suicide and madness will recover their balance, once more go forward, and march proudly in the great procession of the awakened nation.

But Fanon went further in his analysis when he argued that the imperialists have been able to use the Lumpenproletariat against the national liberation struggle. Fanon reasoned that if the forces of rebellion do not quickly organize the Lumpenproletariat they would fight together as "hired soldiers with the colonial troops." At this point, Fanon cited many examples to buttress his theory: the harkis and messalists were used by the French against the Algerian Liberation forces; the "roadopeners" who preceded the Portuguese armed columns in Angola; the organized demonstrations of separatists in Kasai and Katanga in Congo; the "spontaneous participants" in the mass meetings against Lumumba in Leopoldville, and perhaps the utilization of the Zulus by the apartheid regime of the Republic of South Africa against Mandela. Fanon contended that it was not surprising that the Lumpenproletariat, who was characterized by spiritual instability, were used to achieve the goals of imperialism. The Lumpenproletariat consisted of individuals "whose participation is constantly at the mercy of their being for too long accustomed to physiological wretchedness, humiliation, and irresponsibility" (Fanon, 1963: 110). Many capable scholars have amply dissected Fanon's works.

Fanon identified and added the intelligentsia and the national bourgeoisie to the structures of terrorism. Fanon (1963: 116) argued, that the "wily intellectuals, those spoilt children of yesterday's colonialism and of today's national governments organize the loot of whatever national resources exist. Without pity, they use today's national distress as a means of getting on through scheming and legal robbery, by import-export combines, limited liability companies, gambling on the stock exchange, or unfair promotion." Fanon claimed that the intellectuals in Africa lacked the resolve they need, and he blamed it on the indigenous bourgeoisie. He argued that in order to prevent economic decline, corruption, regime of tyranny, force and intimidation, and achieve progress, the road to bourgeoisie must be blocked.

Also, in examining the function of the national bourgeoisie, Fanon (1963: 142) argued as follows:

> The national middle-class, which takes over power at the end of the colonial regime, is an underdeveloped middle-class. It has practically no economic power, and in any case it is in no way commensurate with the bourgeoisie of the mother country which it hopes to replace.... The university and merchant classes which make up the most enlightened section of the new state are in fact characterized by the smallness number and their being concentrated in the capital, and in the type of activities in which they are engaged; business, agriculture, and the liberal professions. Neither financiers nor industrial magnates are to be found within this national middle class. The national bourgeoisie of underdeveloped countries is not engaged in production, nor in invention, nor building, nor labor; it is completely canalized into activities of the intermediary type. Its innermost vocation seems to be to keep in the running and to be part of the racket. The psychology of the national bourgeoisie is that of the business man, not that of the captain of industry; and it is only too true that the greed of the settlers and the system of embargoes set up by colonialism has hardly left them any further choice.

In short, Fanon argued that what Africa has is a weak national capitalist, a middleman or a representative of the big foreign companies. The national bourgeoisie only functions as imperialism's internal ally in the post-independence game of neocolonialism. The peripheral capitalists, in Fanon's view, make no effort to improve or change the economy. He is content with producing raw materials for export to core countries. To Fanon, the African bourgeois was a greedy, gluttonous "huckster," who is indebted with whatever resources that the core power hands out. Fanon concluded that no true bourgeoisie exists in Africa.

Political Repression

According to a powerful African scholar, imperialism, colonialism, and neocolonialism have created different social classes, especially the petty and comparador bourgeoisie, who have vested interests in a system of national economic dependence and continued poverty of the masses (Ake, 1978). The political disempowerment of the masses contributes to their economic dependency. Third world nations (e.g., Kenya, Zaire) are characterized by political tin gods, life-presidents, military regimes, one-party systems, arrest and detention without trial of political opponents, the disappearance of political dissenters, and billionaire presidents (Ake, 1978). Most African nations exhibit these characteristics either singly or in various combinations. In some countries, which allow pseudo-democratic participation by the masses, political parties are not designed to alleviate poverty and the suffering of the masses. When the people's loyalty is in doubt, intimidation through the use or threat of violence, blackmail, bribery, and election rigging are quickly called into action. Such acts of domestically targeted state terrorism are an integral part of neo-colonial, peripheral politics (Ake, 1978; Gamer, 1983).

Arbitrariness in the exercise of power replaces respect for the people. "Life presidents" trust only themselves, family relatives and a gang of "petty bourgeois sycophants and philistines" (Ake 1978). Citizens become objects of control, manipulation and intimidation. The leader abdicates the search for legitimacy and instead, relies on lies, intimidation, blackmail, bribery and naked force. Political dissenters are terrorized and crushed. Rivals are liquidated and soon after are presumed dead. Intellectuals are sent letter bombs. The people dissolve into indolence and lethargy (Ake, 1978). Anyone who opposes the leader or stands up for democratic principles or for the truth becomes an enemy and must be bought or destroyed. This is terrorism at its best in the WS. The greedy attitudes of the rulers result in economic terrorism engendered by economic repression.

Economic Repression/Terrorism

The peripheral bourgeoisie, (especially African bourgeoisie) suffers from many weaknesses attributed to a colonial legacy. One of its crucial weaknesses is the lack of a strong material base. To briefly illustrate, under colonialism, natives were not allowed to have access to wealth. The most productive land in Kenya was reserved for the European settlers. As in the Republic of South Africa, a combination of legal sanctions forced Africans out of these productive lands (Gamer, 1983).

In Africa, Latin America, and Asia the trend was the same. Land was under the private control of commercial profits (Gamer, 1983). Exportation of crops to core states was emphasized while sustenance crops were ignored. This resulted in the disintegration of clans and communities. Many citizens were deliberately forced out of their communities. Many were terrorized and killed. According to Gammer (1983), in the Caribbean, the few original American Indian inhabitants who constituted the only remnants of "traditional village structure were massacred or moved." Sugar cane estates subsequently replaced them or African slaves. Under colonial policies such as those produced in post-independence Africa, a vulnerable small bourgeoisie with a very weak material base emerges (Gamer, 1983).

The important question to be answered, then, is how then can the national bourgeoisie of a peripheral country strengthen its material base? In an effort to provide solutions to this issue, the concept of economic terrorism emerges. Economic terrorism involves the expropriation of peripheral funds or money to the core countries, which leads to violence in the peripheral countries. The ruling class inciting one group against the other as the cause of the peripheral economic decline also characterizes it. Violence emerges in the form of one religious group against another, or one ethnic group against another apportioning blames indiscriminately. By trying to strengthen its material base, the national capitalists must find other effective mechanisms of exploitation aside from the established methods of colonial management (Ake, 1978).

One of the methods is the direct use of coercive power for the expropriation of labor. What is happening in peripheral Africa today is identical to what Marx labeled as primitive accumulation (the direct use of coercion to appropriate economic surplus or the means of production). In West African countries where economic terrorism or sabotage is evident, the direct use of coercive power sometimes takes the form of political conflict. Citizens are denounced for some political crime and then are murdered or imprisoned and there property seized. Sometimes people in peripheral societies are accused of being unpatriotic and subversive, or of economic exploitation of other groups, and popular animosity is built against them. What follows such situations, under cover of political conflict is extreme violence and abuse that may sometimes lead to mass genocide, as was the case in Rwanda. Globally, Iraq's massacre of the Kurds provides additional example. Other examples exist in West African countries such as Nigeria, Cameroon and Ghana that have embarked in such terrorist tactics in their history.

If the argument above is correct, then coercive accumulation depletes the number of citizens in peripheral societies who have the ability and native talent to make their economic system creative. Most importantly, the use of violence/terrorism to expropriate resources from other members of the ruling class may escalate the level of insecurity within the whole class structure. This leads to a vicious circle of terrorism. Because of such political power struggles development suffers. Under such a climate, neither culture nor industry can be encouraged (Ake, 1978).

Another policy that the peripheral bourgeoisie uses to maintain its material base is to apply political pressures against the core agents operating in peripheral societies (Ake, 1978). In many countries such as Nigeria, Kenya, and Tanzania, indigenization programs were designed to pressure imperialist agents as well as to consolidate political powers. These pressures take many forms. Sometimes peripheral rural class leaders demand a greater share of the economic surplus. Most importantly, peripheral bourgeoisie endeavor to solicit nationalist feelings against foreign capital, and seek partnerships in their business enterprises (Ohaegbulam, 1977). Finally, in most African nations the military acts as ruler. This means that African countries are characterized by "booty capitalism" which is not conducive to economic development. The point is that many regimes rely on force to ensure widespread compliance and to control economic distribution of the surplus.

There is the tendency not only to use force in political battles, but also to appropriate surplus by force. As with the civilian governments, whose ministers loot African resources and export African money abroad, the new military regime also allows its leadership to use instruments of violence to become capitalists. The military officers at the lower end of the administrative echelon became angry at the way the country's wealth is being hoarded by the top officials. They too want some of the national cake. This situation may result in a coup, which may lead to violence. The vicious circle of extremism, terrorism, and political violence emerges again. And regardless of who is in charge, the economy is still dependent on foreign economies (Gamer, 1983; Ake, 1978).

The point is that the peripheral bourgeoisie do not place emphasis on food production, the provision of rural and urban housing, and the manufacture of drugs or correcting the poor supply of water, and poor street lighting and so on (Jaffe, 1985). The poor majority in both the urban and rural areas live under conditions of everlasting austerity which is not conducive to peace, justice and security. Ake (1978) indicated that most of them lack access to elementary social activities (e.g., social security, food stamps, credit facilities, simple recreational activities for children, power delivery, and telephones). In the face of all these limitations, the masses are faced with the contradiction that the members of the ruling class have billions of dollars in foreign banks and live sumptuous lives. By following the ideology of development, the ruling class and the national bourgeoisie create more problems than they can handle. The persistence of underdevelopment, especially extreme poverty in peripheral societies, constitutes a leading cause of economic terrorism and violence in general.

Peripheral societies may not realize the goal of development unless they decolonize the structures of imperialism. They may consider the path of classical capitalism of Adam Smith's *Wealth of Nations* not colonial capitalism. For classical capitalism, the principle of laisser-faire was significant because competition was emphasized (Ake, 1978). Competition was viewed as the only economic system, which will serve the best interest of the people. Although, competition may lead to waste, misallocation, anarchy in production and monopoly, capitalism, despite Marx's critiques, constituted the most important revolutionary effect in changing and expanding the forces of production in Western Europe. If handled well, capitalism may lead to economic development (Ake, 1978).

On the other hand, the same argument cannot be made of colonial capitalism. A colonial power that rules by force cannot encourage the principle of laisser faire (see Ake, 1978; Gamer, 1983; Omer-Cooper, 1986). Rather, it creates and sustains a peripheral dependent economy that is externally oriented. Such dependent economies de-emphasized competition and allowed the centralization of capital in peripheral societies. Competition might enable the indigenous people to acquire wealth, become successful and gain political power despite its inherent exploitations. Such advantages might endanger the core power in the periphery. It might also undermine the imperial principle, which represents peripheral societies as less than human in order to justify their inhumane treatment. Colonial policies were aimed at denying colonized peoples access to economic development and to maintain their conditions of wretchedness (Gamer, 1983).

In short, colonial capitalism is more interested in external demand than internal demand. It is not interested in transportation systems that will advance the quality of life of the colonized people. It is interested in building and maintaining roads that will transport peripheral products and raw materials to the center countries. It encourages education but emphasizes only that part of learning (interpreters, maids, nurses, clerks, etc.,) that will help core officials discharge their official duties effectively and efficiently. Colonial capitalism inhibits the development of technology, and disallows the colonies from turning primary products into manufactured goods (Ake, 1978). It encourages devaluation of native currencies. Colonial capitalism succeeded in Africa and other sections of the world by using repressive methods to carry out its objectives. Violence was used to create and sustain colonial capitalism in peripheral societies (Ake, 1978).

The colonizers need a peripheral supply of labor to carry out the exploitation of the colony. In order to achieve this goal, coercion must be employed. People are rounded up and terrorized to build railways, roads, gather raw materials and prepare them for export. Simply put, men and women are terrorized to work and to pay taxes for the money economy. The violence, which results from the antagonism between the rich and poor nations, has often led to external interventions in post-colonial independence (Gamer, 1983; Ake, 1978).

External Intervention

The aim of this section is to look at external intervention as an addition to the factors that direct structural violence in peripheral societies with particular emphasis on Africa. External intervention arises at two different phases in Africa: one occurs with respect to conflicts concerning two internal factions in an African nation. The other emanates in conflicts between one African country and another. Most of these conflicts are characterized by military takeover of power (Mazrui and Tidy, 1984).

The problem again rests on colonial exploitation, neocolonialism and other pertinent factors, which prevent post-independent African states from producing goods, and services, which are needed to satisfy the minimum expectations of the masses. One may expect the new rulers of Africa (after independence) to abandon or abolish exploitative economic relations and to redistribute African wealth for the betterment of the material conditions of the masses. Such was not the case after independence, and such is not the case today.

Instead, the pressures were too much on the rulers to the extent that they could not resolve the problems of authority and integration. They decided to maintain the colonial legacy, that is, sustain the exploitative relations and a stratification system, which is dominated by the privileged stratum. They refused to restructure the economy and abandon demands for mass participation in both political and economic circles of the society (Ake, 1978; Gamer, 1983). Consequently, dissident groups, political opponents and progressives are terrorized, intimidated and murdered. Public outcry against the use of terrorism/violence by the ruling elite against the "wretched of the earth" may lead to either foreign intervention (imperial powers) or an African country intervening in the internal affairs of another African country as shall be demonstrated.

The threats to peace, security and development in Africa caused by colonial rule and economic dependency are unique and part of the reasons core powers intervene in African affairs. For example, France intervened in the 1980s in Chad and the Central African Republic through the employment of open military force. In Angola, between 1975-76, core powers intervened through covert military oppression. In both instances the interest of the core countries was to prevent a threat to western raw material supplies and investments, to maintain a satellite regime in power and to avert socialist influence in the former colonial regions (Mazrui and Tidy, 1984).

The tendency of the core states to continue to control the affairs of the peripheral states (African nations) and the desire of African rulers to remain in power at all costs (e.g., Mobutu Seku Toure in Zaire) demonstrates external intervention in the internal conflicts of a peripheral state. One example is the arbitrary boundaries created by the colonial powers that were not based on race, religion, language and culture. In many African countries these boundaries have created and reinforced conflict and instability. Nigeria, Zaire, Sudan, and Uganda have all experienced crises caused by colonial boundaries (Gamer, 1983). As a result external interventions have been common in these nations. Yugoslavia is experiencing the same fate but instead has engaged in ethnic cleansing of its population.

Socialist countries have also intervened in internal conflicts of African countries. For example, in the 1970s, the former Soviet Union intervened in the Nigerian civil war on behalf of the Federal authorities.

The Nigerian authorities to crush the spirits of the opposition utilized Soviet technology of violence. However, socialist countries claim that their intervention in African internal affairs is in direct response to revolutionary pressures as they arise due to Africa's underdevelopment and dependency. In short, they do not claim that intervention is characterized by their desire to control the client state's economy or to protect their economic interests and investments (Galan, 1990).

Core powers have often intervened in inter-state conflicts in Africa in favor of satellite states against the emergence of radically oriented governments. Socialist nations tend to intervene in order to support radically oriented regimes against the existing state's authority (Bulham, 1985). Numerous examples are available for illustration. Morocco's desire to annex Western Sahara against the wishes of the Polisario Front because of Morocco's pro-West role in relation to the Middle East and the progressive nature of Western Sahara was supported by the West. In the Ogaden conflict between Ethiopia and Somalia, the U.S.A. supported Somalia because of its key military and geographic significance to the Persian Gulf coupled with its anti-socialism, against Ethiopia's radical anti-imperialism, and ties to the former Soviet Union. The Libyan and Egyptian conflict saw the U.S.A. taking an aggressive policy against Libyan radicalism in favor of Egyptian moderate policy toward the Middle Eastern crisis. Also, the USA's hostility against Libya during the Reagan administration led to the bombing of Tripoli due to Libya's involvement in international terrorism in April of 1935 (see Perdue, 1989; Mazrui and Tidy, 1986).

African countries have also been involved in other African nation's domestic affairs. The recent example is Nigeria's intervention in the Liberian conflict in the 1990s as well as Nigerian participation in Somalia conflicts and Sierra Leone. Other examples include the Ivory Coast's attempt to disrupt its radical neighbors in the 1960s. Tanzania fully participated in Uganda by removing Idi Amin from power. Senegal also intervened in Gambia whereas Libya attempted to destabilize the government of Chad (Mazrui and Tidy, 1984). European's technology of violence has armed African states so dangerously that African interventions in the internal conflicts of other states are now very likely (Mazrui and Tidy, 1986).

In short, external intervention either by foreign powers or by African states has contributed significantly to structural terrorism in Africa. This is made possible by external powers arming different states in Africa with dangerous weapons. These various forms of interventions disrupt peace, security, and development. The core's participation in arming peripheral nations with massive technology of weapons weakens the peripheral economy, prolongs violence, and reinforces dependence on center countries (Mazrui and Tidy, 1984). Rather than avoiding violence, the weapons of destruction made available to peripheral countries by core nations destroys the desire for compromise thereby encouraging full-blown violence in these third world nations. Simply put, by supplying weapons of violence to poor countries, a structure of violence and repression, which undermines economic progress, political participation (e.g. self confidence of peripheral population) is created. Countries such as those in the Middle East may use these weapons to engage in international terrorism. However, West African countries do not participate in international terrorism as the next section illustrates.

The Effects of Colonialism and Why West African Countries Have Not Participated in International Terrorism

West African countries are not immune from engaging in terrorism (Denmark and Welfling, 1988). Terrorism occurs in West African countries but not in the same magnitude as it occurs in other parts of the world (Denmark and Welfling, 1988) that experienced the same debilitating effects of the colonial economic policies. What follows is a brief discussion of the colonial economy, results, and policies.

The Colonial Economy, Results and Policies in West African Countries

This book has consistently condemned colonial capitalism because of its emphasis on the West Africa's economy supply of labor. Colonial capitalism used coercion and naked force to exploit the natural resources of West African states. It encouraged the exportation of African crops to the core countries and discouraged internal industrialization of West Africa. It has also been proposed earlier that what is needed in West Africa is a new economic system, perhaps a new free enterprise system that will encourage native talents, local participation, and local industries. This argument is not radically different from the position taken in chapter one by Cardoso for Latin American countries.

In West Africa, the British and French policies regarding the economic development were very identical in practice. Each of the core powers used violence to produce raw materials for their home industries. Their economic policies in West Africa were very egocentric and were designed to profit the colonial powers (Ake, 1978; Gamer, 1983; Coleman, 1960; Hodgkin, 1957; Mazrui and Tidy, 1984; Asante, 1983; Denmark and Welfling, 1983). In short, these powers were not interested in establishing industries in their West African territories. Cocoa, timber, palm oil, groundnuts, leather, cotton and rubber were grown in West Africa and sold at very cheap prices to European corporations. The core powers promoted the export of these crops but never supported the production of domestically consumed staple foods that include yams, cassava, millet, and other locally produced food items (Gamer, 1983).

It can then be argued that these core powers deliberately were interested in those policies that would help them realize their economic objectives. They quickly prohibited "trade by barter" as well as traditional currencies that existed in West Africa before European settlers. They also designed a system of communication and forcefully introduced their own currencies for quicker economic transactions. The railways were constructed for specific purposes. For example, the Y-shaped railway system of Sierra Leone tapped the palm oil producing regions of the country. It also allowed the core powers to move their military and police to regions where colonial policies were challenged by force of arms (Gamer, 1983; Ake, 1978; Coleman, 1950).

These European powers believed that Africans were lazy (Coleman, 1950). Although this is Eurocentric nonsense, they directly and indirectly forced, recruited and controlled labor since it was essential to build colonial roads and railways. In fact, many African scholars have written that these powers relied on colonial laws and regulations which coerced West African chiefs to recruit their subjects to work even against their will on colonial projects such as carrying the European administrator and his belongings or the luggage of the military and the police from one place to another (Gamer, 1983; Onwubiko 1975; Ohaegbulam, 1977).

The core powers also introduced a rigid system of taxation that led to riots and uprisings in the southern states of Nigeria. Some basic education that was introduced by the powers was liberal with religious legitimization. This religious education was aimed to indoctrinate the oppressed to accept the colonial policies. Although railways and roads were built for reasons already expressed, Britain and France did nothing else of permanent importance to encourage economic development in

West Africa (Mazrui, 1977). And it is for these reasons that I have argued for the abandonment of colonial economic system in West Africa. The results of these economic policies rest on the premises that the colonial governments remained basically unable to provide adequate social services for the people. Hospitals and schools were illequipped, many areas lacked roads, railways were built for particular purposes, and people of different cultures were forced to stay in one country creating more problems in West Africa (Ake, 1978; Coleman, 1950).

Despite these colonial policies West African countries, unlike Middle-Eastern and Asian nations, have maintained good relationships with these powers. West African leaders have consistently sought to improve relations with the core powers and have refused to engage or promote international terrorism for several reasons. These include the resilience of tradition, domestic responses to revolutionary pressures, military intervention, and the technology of violence. Each of these reasons is discussed more fully below.

The Resilience of Tradition

It is true that many African traditions felt the influence of colonial domination. However, Africa is still characterized by "a theme of resilience and durability" (Mazrui, 1977). Traditionalism (the doctrines or practices of those who follow or accept tradition) is unique to Africans because it links Africans to their pre-colonial past and maintains the dominance of roots. Traditionalists oppose radicalism and even modernism, and if change is to occur it must respond fully to the lessons of the past. Terrorism in the WS is a radical departure from African values. It goes against African values, tribal norms and cultural nationalism. African leaders were much more interested in gaining political independence than in terrorizing their colonial masters (for full discussion of this concept, see Mazrui 1977).

Domestic Responses to Revolutionary Pressures

Another reason why West African nations have not engaged in international terrorism is because of the African bourgeoisies' response to revolutionary pressures at home. Domestic or economic terrorism is enough pressure on the African ruling class. It makes no sense to participate in external terrorism. Ake (1978) suggested that there are strong revolutionary pressures against the maintenance of the present exploitative class relations and pressures against the existence of the African bourgeois class. These pressures arise, Ake (1978:77) argued from: the desperate poverty of the African masses; the sharp and highly visible differences between the rich and the poor; rising expectations associated with modernization; the example of developed countries, made even more effective by their penetration of the periphery; and the politicization of the popular consciousness by the nationalist movement and by the dynamics of contradictions between the metropolitan bourgeoisie and the African bourgeoisie. These revolutionary pressures occupy ruling class attention. Consequently, the ruling class has much to do at home to insure that they maintain their positions of power. With much of their time devoted to maintaining domestic peace, the African ruling class has little time to seek it's own independence from colonial regimes. It is also in the best interest of the African ruling class not to engage in international terrorism due to their position of power in the WS. Largely, colonized ruling classes are sheltered into the WS, and much of their power, privilege and prestige come from their association with the colonizers.

Military Intervention

Okwudiba (1985) claims that since 1960 three out of five countries in North Africa, ten out of fifteen in West Africa, and seven out of eight in central Africa have been under military rule at least once. Anyan'nyong'o (1986) argued that coup d'etat--the sudden and swift overthrow of a sitting government through the use of, or threat of force--is the most frequent form of military takeover of governments in Africa. Another form of military intervention occurs when a foreign power through the use or threat of armed might, intervenes in the internal politics of a sovereign African state to save a sister state from being overthrown (Nyong'o, 1986). A third type of military intervention occurs when imperialist and sub-imperialist powers systematically try to recruit and maintain a repressive regime in Africa.

Mazrui and Tidy (1984) gave their own reasons why military intervention occurs in Africa. They asserted that the most common factors that lead to military coup d'etat are:

> Inadequate preparations for independence by the colonial powers, a misuse of Western European models of government and an emphasis on party politics rather than mobilization for national needs; corruption among the ruling civilian elite; and acute economic crisis; the prevalence and even the worsening of regionalism and ethnicism; military discontent with the general situation in the country; threats to the position of the military; and the relative ease of a physical take over of government by the military (Mazrui and Tidy, 1984:227).

The coup d'etat takes place within the auspices of the neocolonial state and provides no avenues for structural change (Ake, 1978). For example, Nigeria had its first coup in January 1966 and a second coup in July1966 and continues to have military takeovers without any economically innovative ideas. Ghana's first coup took place in 1966 and a second coup in 1972. There were subsequent coups in 1978, 1979, and 1981. Liberia has its own share of coup d'etat in 1980 and continues to have political and economic turmoil (Mazrui and Tidy, 1984). The point is that internal terrorism already exists in West African internal politics that makes external terrorism a rarity.

Technology of Violence

It can be argued that terrorism is less pervasive in Africa than in the core areas of the world (Denemark and Welfling, 1988). At the same time, it is not true that Africans tolerated European intrusion without struggle. In fact, Europeans met brave resistance at the hands of the West African peoples (Mazrui, 1977). However, lacking the material and human resources, political elite in Africa is not capable of solving some of the fundamental problems facing the masses. Political and military leaders can only inflict a regime of terror internally and cannot afford to waste resources externally.

The argument is that African leaders lack the technology of violence needed to fight against colonialism. The phrase technology of violence means the invention and improvement of global weapons of destruction (Mazrui, 1977). An advanced technology of violence is unique to the Europeans and even the Middle Eastern areas of Africa. There are the Europeans who make these weapons of destruction and the

Arabs who can afford to buy them and in turn use them against the Western people. West Africans on the other hand, have massive economic problems at home and may not afford the development and purchase of these weapons. And even in today's society many African countries lack the sophisticated weapons that are common in the streets of the western world. The terror of gunfire was a European product. Mazrui (1977:46) provides an excellent explanation:

> The terror of gunfire lay in the superior military technology which western man brought with him as an argument in the quest for allegiance and annexation in the African continent. Gunfire was demonstrated to those as yet unconvinced of their own vulnerability. Some bought guns of their own, especially in West Africa, and attempted to confront the European invader with his own weapons. Other groups elsewhere relied on antiquated military technology of spears against the devastation of the Maxim gun. Still others capitulated not because they themselves had suffered the humiliating destructive power of Europe's technology of violence, but because they had heard enough from neighboring communities about this power to give up in despair beforehand.... In time the fear of hell-fire accompanied this dread of gunfire. The fear of hell-fire was in part a ritualization of terror.

Conclusion

Fanon's theory of violence was used to connect terrorism to the WST. A structural theory of terrorism based on colonialism, neocolonialism, and imperialism was developed and it was suggested that peace, security and development are threatened in peripheral nations due to these structures. Moreover, West African countries, particularly affected by these structures have not been interested in international terrorism due to their traditional submissiveness to their culture. Finally, criminological theories were examined and found to be deficient in the explanation of international patterns of criminality and terrorism. It was suggested that criminologists embrace WST in order to expand their knowledge about crime and terrorism rather than being isolated from the world in which they live. The next chapter will examine the data and methodology used in the literature in studying terrorism and WST.

4. Data Methods

Introduction

This chapter reviews methods of measuring WS position and terrorism incidents. Other scholars generally have used the block model analysis of Snyder and Kick's (1979) as the basis for WS classifications. Thus, Snyder and Kick's research will be the starting point for measuring WS position. However, Snyder and Kick's classification has also been criticized (Bollen 1983; Jackman 1980) and suggestions for a better method, which would eliminate misclassifications of countries, shall also be reviewed. The point is that there is no one acceptable measurement of WS positions. It will be demonstrated in this descriptive analysis different views on how WS position has been measured by different scholars. Also, included in this chapter is a discussion of measurement issues related to attempts to record terrorism. Various terrorism databases are reviewed. Finally, the distribution of terrorism by WS position is compiled from these data.

World System Position: An Overview

The problem with studying WST and even dependency theory is that scholars who are interested in these subjects do not, "speak with a single voice." Another inherent problem is that WS and dependency scholars have concentrated on the examination of economic growth, and development, and income inequality (Bollen, 1983). Taken independently, such studies and measures are inconsistent with the broader perspective offered by WS classifications.

Measurement Issues

This section reviews measurement issues pertinent to determining WS position and various methods for classifying a nation's WS position. WS scholars employ different methods of measurement that characterize their perspectives (Portes, 1976; Cardoso, 1977; Smith 1979). No individual researcher has fully embraced another writer's methodological argument (Jackman, 1980; Nolan 1983; Bollen 1983; Snyder and Kicks 1979). However, Snyder and Kick's (1979) block model classification has been adopted by many researchers to measure a nation's position in the WS. Snyder and Kick used the block model analysis to classify countries into core, periphery and semiperiphery.

Snyder and Kick's study looked at trade flows, treaty memberships, military interventions, and diplomatic relations as four types of international networks. Using nation-states as the units of analysis, they concluded, "block model analysis of social structure through multiple networks address WS formulations far more appropriately" (Snyder and Kicks, 1979: 1096). They found support for the WS argument that countries outside the core have experienced lower rates of economic growth and development than core societies.

In their study, Snyder and Kick operationally defined the structure of the WS based on the four international networks already identified. The authors placed emphasis on the organization, sources, and coding methods for every network data obtained. Distinct N X N matrices for each country delineate the four networks. An "I" in the appropriate cell of the matrix designate each tie between nations. The absence of a tie is coded "0". Their analysis was limited to data collected for 1955 to 1970 for 118 countries. For further details concerning the construction of the matrices, see Snyder and Kick (1979: 1105-1106).

Snyder and Kick (1979) and Wallerstein (1974) emphasized that there are no firm empirical criteria for placing countries in their different locations in the WS structure. This means that empirical evidence or appropriate method for classifying countries is still fragmented and descriptive. In short, there are no exact criteria of classification. WS scholars (Chirot, 1977; Galtung, 1971; Wallerstein, 1974; and Snyder and Kick, 1979) have all admitted problems in specifying countries in their WS positions. For example, Chirot (1977) found it very difficult to locate communist nations in their WS positions. Snyder and Kick argued that there is no rule that a three dimensional model (core, semiperiphery, periphery) represents the operation of the WS in its entirety.

Whatever may be the case; these networks (trade flows, military interventions, diplomatic relations, and conjoint treaty memberships) have been used to locate countries in the WS structure. Secondary school and college enrollments (Snyder and Kick, 1979), energy consumption (Bollen, 1983), and the gini index of inequality (Lynch et. al. N.D.) have also been used in the literature as explanatory variables. Snyder and Kick's empirical evidence utilized "the change in gross national product (GNP) per capita from 1955 to 1970 as the dependent variable." A country is then classified based on its relationship (that is, the international networks) with the United States. For example, based on the amount of foreign aid received, international trade flows or trade links with the U.S., position of importance in international organizations (i.e., the United Nations), and its ability to intervene militarily in other nations affairs determines a nation's location in the WS (Snyder and Kick, 1979; Bollen, 1982).

The linkage between world economic location and rate of economic growth is a controversial one. Jackman (1980) strongly objected to the findings of Snyder and Kick, as well as Chase-Dunn (1975). Jackman criticized Snyder and Kick on the basis that their results may be an artifact of economic growth and their use of GNP per capita differences at two time points. Jackman (1980) suggested these interrelated problems could have been avoided by Snyder and Kick if they had used a continuous measure of economic growth rate. Jackman asserted that despite Snyder and Kick's findings, there is no conclusive evidence of a relationship between world economic position and rate of economic growth. He argued that it is more useful to focus on percentage rates of growth than on differences in raw scores since they are based on standardized observations and are more reliable.

Nolan (1983) lamented Jackman's findings and contended that it is premature to dismiss the findings of Snyder and Kick and other world system theorists. Using the measures suggested by Jackman (1980), Nolan provided additional support that dependency increases income inequality and disrupts economic growth. In other controversial research, Rubinson (1976) (also see Rubinson and Quinlan, 1977) supported the hypothesis that there was higher income inequality in dependent than in developed nations. Weede (1980) challenged this finding by objecting to Rubinson's control for the effects of development on income distribution.

Weede suggested that it is necessary for researchers to use a second-order polynomial model. Weede asserted that Rubinson's use of the log of development was inadequate as a control. But when Weede (1980) tried to replicate Rubinson's (1976) analysis using polynomial controls, none of the regression coefficients for Rubinson's indicators of dependency were significant. Weede, therefore, concluded that Rubinson's findings were the result of his "misspecification" of the economic model. Weede dismissed the hypothesis that a country's economic position in the WS affects economic inequality net of economic development.

Bollen (1983) used partial regression plots and a sample of about 100 countries in his analysis of the relations of political democracy to WS positions and economic development. Bollen suggested that Snyder and Kick's WS measure contains some classification error. While he hopes for a better measurement tool, his research concluded that peripheral and seniperipheral societies are less democratic than core societies and that economic development is directly related to political democracy. Based upon this research, Bollen offered some revisions to be incorporated by future researchers using Snyder and Kick's block model analysis.

In another article, Nolan (1988) evaluated hypotheses obtained from models of fertility and fertility decline to assess the relevance of both WS/dependency theory and ecological-evolutionary theory for the population stages of developing nations. Nolan embarked on this research because the most important drawbacks of WS and dependency theories are their lack of emphasis concerning the function of population growth rates in producing and sustaining underdevelopment in the periphery and semiperiphery nations (Chirot, 1977; Lenski and Lenski, 1982). Nolan (1988) argued that WS/dependency theories would have greater explanatory power if it could be demonstrated that high fertility and rapid population growth are products of economic dependency in the world distribution of power.

Nolan's study was restricted to 46 countries for which complete data were obtained, and was divided into four different stages. First, he evaluated the independent impact of techno-economic heritage and WS position. Second, child mortality, family planning effort, service sector size, and female labor force were used as intervening variables to determine the independent effects of development, techno-economic heritage and dependency. Third, the direct impact of the variables on fertility level was examined. Finally, the net of these controls was tested to determine the direct effects of dependency and techno-economic heritage on fertility change. Nolan also examined total fertility rate taken from Tsui and Bogue (1978) and the crude birth rate obtained from the World Bank (1980; 1982). Both measures are important since they contained a significant amount of information on different aspects of fertility.

In a more recent research, Bradshaw and Huang (1991) concluded that International Monetary Fund (IMF) imposed conditionality on third world nations is the most important obstacle to economic growth. Their cross-national analysis used panel regression to test different relevant variables for a 12-year period by focusing on the newest international debt crisis from 1975 - 1987. They supported the WS argument that growing service payments to IMF constitutes an impediment to economic growth. Moreover, the authors concluded, "investment dependence and international reserves inhibit physical quality of life" (Bradshaw and Huang, 1991: 326).

Finally, Bennett (1991) examined both the Durkheimian and opportunity models by evaluating the effects of level of development and rate of growth on crime rates. The author argued that prior studies only analyzed the development level, not its change. He conducted a longitudinal study, which explored the linkage between developmental change and crime rates. He also controlled possible spurious effects, placing emphasis on regression-base, pooled, time-series analysis.

The Durkheimian model that has been employed by many writers (Krohn, 1978; Messner, 1982; Neuman and Berger, 1988; Shelley, 1981) asserts that the rate of increase in crime has a direct relationship to development. A major criticism of this model is centered on its inherent weakness to forecast accurately the differences in crime rates by crime types (Bennett, 1991). The opportunity model, on the other hand, focuses only on developmental level, while ignoring the rate of change, which is needed to predict crime rates (Bennett, 1991).

Bennett used two control variables often found in the literature to specify the linkage between development and crime, and terrorism is a form of violent crime, which makes this literature pertinent in this study. These variables include urbanization and inequality and are also used in WS operationalization (Hansmann and Quiglev 1982; Kick and Lafree, 1985; Messner, 1982). He employed the economic development and potential offender pool size as additional control variables in this time-series design while obtaining data from the international criminal police organization (Interpol), United Nations (U.N.), World Bank, and International Labor Organization between 1960 and 1984. He concluded that the competing models affect the rate and type of crime without showing strong support for either the Durkheimian or opportunity model. In short, the opportunity model explains theft trends, but neither model explains outcomes strongly in the countries studied.

One thing common with these writers, including Immanuel Wallerstein, is their constant call for a future model that would appropriately classify a country's WS position for reasons already discussed. Most authors emphasized that their studies had major limitations due to missing data or mixed results, which added fuel to the controversy over suitable measures and their effects. The major issue is whether or not non-core status in the world economic order does indeed retard, accelerate, or not affect a nation's economic growth and development. Since almost all the researchers face one kind of measurement error or another, there is still an urgent need for alternative classification schemes to place countries into their WS positions. For now, Snyder and Kick's (1979) blockmodel classification model is the best there is, and cannot be dismissed until a better measurement approach is designed. What follows is the list of countries in their WS positions.

Listing of Societies in the World System by Status

This section specifically reviews research on classifying nations in WS position. This review begins with Snyder and Kick's (1979: 1110) recommendation on assigning nations to a WS location. A simplified version of Snyder and Kick's block model is found in Table 2. It contains countries and their classifications in the WS core-periphery-semiperiphery structure. For example, Core societies are represented by nations such as the U.S. Canada, U.S.S.R. and Israel belong to the semiperiphry zone, while Cameroon and Nicaragua are in the periphery. Bollen (1983) argued that Snyder and Kick's (1979) block model analysis accommodated classification error. While Bollen offered useful revisions, he did not suggest alternative measurement tools other than those of Snyder and Kick. In fact, Jackman (1980) and Weede (1980) in their criticisms did not suggest alternative measurement strategies. However, Bollen's revisions are important to note in the present day classifications of countries into their WS positions.

Bollen asserted, "position in the WS is largely a relational concept" (1983: 474). Nations of the same status have certain characteristics in common. For example, a core country such as the U.S.

is more likely to be economically diversified, influential in world political circles and highly industrialized. Such a country is not likely to receive foreign economic assistance from other countries. It is also a militarily powerful nation. It is likely for such a country to have substantial control in the international organizations in which it is a member (e.g., NATO or the United Nations). In Bollen's view, these characteristics apply only to a very few countries such as the United States and United Kingdom. Therefore, Spain, Portugal and South Africa must not be classified (as in Snyder and Kick, 1979) as belonging to the core areas of the world. Bollen argued also that, Taiwan, Iraq, and Saudi Arabia were in the periphery in the 1960s not the semiperiphery. Bollen (1983) offered different reasons to substantiate his position. The point is that writers of the WS should include Bollen's revisions (Lynch et al. N.D.).

In this case, it is not correct to rank countries based only on their economic and political relationships with the U.S. Most countries such as the former U.S.S.R. and China belonged to the communist international hemisphere. Their political climate and associations preclude them from establishing significant trade relations with the U.S. and their Western allies. The Cold War provides an illustration of this dilemma. The cold war was fought primarily between the U.S. and the Soviet Union. The Soviet Union and the U.S. had countries all over the globe under their own wings. For example, in Ethiopia, Somalia and other countries, both U.S. and the U.S.S.R. supported different factions and equipped them with munitions. Such political and military support demonstrates their relative positions of power in the world. Both countries had nuclear weapons that could destroy each other. How then can Snyder and Kick place Sweden, South Africa, Portugal, Luxembourg, etc., in the core areas without including China and the U.S.S.R.?

The argument is simple. Snyder and Kick's classifications reflect only Eurocentric measurement of a countrys' positions of power in the WS. The black African nations, although friendly with the U.S., were all classified as belonging to the periphery with the exception of Kenya in the semiperiphery. At least, Nigeria, otherwise known as the giant of Africa, must have been located in the semineriphery (Nolan, 1991). Nigeria is a regional power in Africa. She has sent troops to Liberia, Siera Leone and participated in the U.S. effort to restore peace in Somalia. Nigeria is the second largest supplier of crude oil to the United States. Economically and politically, Nigeria commands international respect and also maintains good relationships with the United States. Nigeria is the recognized voice of Africa in the United Nations.

My suggestion is that countries should be classified in the WS based on their regional distribution of power. Countries cannot be based on their relationship with the U.S. alone or other Eurocentric defined core countries. Unless this is done such countries like Nigeria that command respect in the organization of African Unity (O.A.U.) and Economic Community of West African States (ECOWAS), to name but a few, would always be misclassified by the WS theorists. It is this kind of regional power that translates into world power in international organizations such as the UN.

Based on these premises, it is absurd to rank Spain who was denied membership in NATO (Bollen 1983) as a core nation. Until other measures are designed, countries, in my opinion, should be classified based on their regional trade and diplomatic relationships with one another. One wonders why only European countries were widely represented in the core. The argument about placing Nigeria in the semiperiphery zone is supported by Nolan (1991). Nolan recognized Nigeria as a strong, semiperipheral nation as the following table illustrates (see Table 3). The table delineates Nigeria and other countries such as Ghana, Zaire, Kenya, and Zambia in the semiperiphery zone. Only nations in the semiperiphery block are represented as being strong or weak. In Nolan's (1991) cross-classifications these countries are placed in the periphery block.

Nolan (1983) and Lynch et al. (N.D.) have also offered their own reclassification suggestions. Furthermore, based upon shifts in the world order that have occurred during the 1980s, additional modifications to Snyder and Kick's model appear to be in order. Table 4 thus contains WS position based upon Snyder and Kick's model with amendments offered by Bollen (1983), Nolan (1991) and Lynch et al. (N.D.). Table 4 is the current classification of countries in their WS positions. These classifications shall be employed to assess how terrorism is distributed throughout the world, and the relationship between terrorism and WS position. In table 4, South Africa has been moved from the core zone to the semiperipheral block, while Nigeria shifted from its peripheral location to semiperipheral status. As the table illustrates, many other countries have also changed positions in their WS periphery-semiperiphery-core structure. Table 4 is very important since WS scholars including Bollen, Nolan, and Lynch et al. (N.D.) have amended Snyder and Kick's (1979) original classifications.

Having examined the measurement of WS location and demonstrating the position of various nations in the WS, the next section turns to an assessment of terrorism data and the measurement of terrorism.

Measurement of Terrorism and Terrorism Data

Like WS position, the measurement of terrorism has been difficult. The term terrorism originated in France during Robespierre's Reign of Terror (Wardlaw, 1986). Since then, terrorism has become an inevitable part of modern life. For example, states such as the Soviet Union (Ludwwikowski, 1988) or former South Africa have employed terrorist acts of violence to achieve political goals. Different anarchist groups in the 19th and 20th centuries in Europe, Latin America, the Middle East, Africa and other parts of the world have also adopted terrorism to attain certain political objectives. Academics and scholars (Gurr 1979; 1972; 1980; 1985; Eckstein 1980; 1972, 1965) have long engaged in the study of problems identical to terrorism in the form of guerrilla warfare, insurrections, revolutions, limited wars, rebellions and insurgencies.

There is disagreement over the definition of terrorism as reviewed in chapter two, which constitutes a major drawback to the development of research on terrorism. Scholars have tried to study terrorism separately from internal wars and guerrilla warfare (Crenshaw, 1992; Miller, 1988; Hoffman, 1992). Most studies on the problem of terrorism are mainly explained by their titles. However, this extensive literature fails to provide reliable information on political, international, and domestic terrorism and its consequences to the modern world.

Since the issue of terrorism attracts the attention of policy makers and a larger population of society, there is an overflow of information, which has escaped scholarly categorization and order, resulting in some difficulties in research and analysis. Crenshaw (1992) stated that "the study of terrorism ... is widely recognized as theoretically impoverished." She maintains that the surveys of research on political violence have historically neglected terrorism. One problem is that the definition of what constitutes political terrorism is inherently ambiguous (Crenshaw, 1992; Miller, 1988; Hoffman, 1992). Terrorism is difficult to study because it embraces various forms and levels of political violence. It does not "present a neater or more homogeneous category of empirical events" (Crenshaw 1992:3).

Methodological Issues

Gurr (1988) identified several databases that emerge when empirically analyzing terrorism such as the civil strife database, the New York Times supplemented by regional news sources, and the scholarly literature. Gurr also asserted that a thorough knowledge of any subject requires a multidisciplinary approach. Data on terrorism events for groups and state actions are, perhaps, the most useful in selecting broad trends and patterns. These data are useful for testing macro-theories about terrorism (Eulau, 1967).

Ross (1988) argued that events data make it possible for researchers to study the terrorist's behavior, using the discrete incident as the unit of analysis. The discrete incident is a better and more reliable measure than statements made by observers and practitioners in the field. A discrete random variable takes on only a finite (or countable) number of values.

While Ross (1988) asserted that discrete incidents are the best form of data on terrorism, many scholars have criticized the use of events data. Doran et al. (1973) questioned their reliability and validity, and Burgess (1975) attacks their relevance to policy analysis because they only provide a sketch, not a specifically accurate portrayal of the more serious political terrorism that occurs in the world today. Burgess contended that most events data research is purely atheoretical. Various organizations, agencies, and institutes have engaged in the business of monitoring terrorism. Schmid (1983) provided a complete review of the databases.

Sources of Data Collection

Some sources of information on terrorist activity include the U.S. Central Intelligence Agency (CIA), the U.S. Department of State data, and the RAND Chronology of International Terrorism. The CIA data base, which includes the Department of State documents trends on terrorism, are based on an analysis of terrorist activity broken down by location, times, number of victims, type of action, and nationality of perpetrators and targets. The RAND Chronology, which shall be discussed in detail in the next section, extends its breakdown of events to the type of tactics used by the terrorists. Separate from the agency monitoring of international terrorism, there are prior studies that have concentrated on specific forms of terrorism. Holden (1986) obtained data from the Federal Aviation Administration (FAA) in his research on the contagiousness of aircraft hijacking and the study of terrorist violence of the Irish Republican Army during 1916-1986.

Mitchell (1985) relied on data from the RAND Corporation, the Federal Bureau of Investigation (FBI), and the CIA in his examination on the incidence of politically motivated insurgent terrorism in North America from 1968 to 1983. He concluded that there is a lack of data on terrorism in Canada. Kelleett (1981) conducted a detailed study of terrorism affecting Canada based on a chronology of international terrorist events affecting Canada between 1968-1979. He asserted that Canada has experienced a relatively low level of international terrorism. These studies are relevant because they included data based on RAND Chronology and they predicted, based on this data that Canada will probably continue to experience a relatively low level of international terrorism. (For details on more measurement issues and how data are gathered, see the next subsection).

Most important, and more relevant to this research, are studies, which have suggested that economic conditions are significant factors in social conflict. These authors argued, based on their quantitative studies, that conflict is more frequent and severe in poor societies than in wealthy nations (Lipset 1960; Gurr 1971; Tilly 1975; Rude 1964). Although these studies tend to argue that adverse economic conditions are linked to the outbreak of violence in several poor countries, none actually measured the direct relationship between WST and terrorism. It is this limitation that will be addressed descriptively in the next chapter. It will be argued that improving the economic conditions of the periphery and semiperiphery nations might reduce terrorist violence. In any situation of structural violence (i.e. violence caused by an asymmetrical power relationship due to injustice, power politics, imperialism, or oppression) the strong use violence against their prey simply by the virtue of being stronger. As argued in chapter three, such violence encourages terrorism as a defensive reaction. However, most weak nations in West Africa do not employ violence as a mechanism of reaction for reasons already articulated.

The Data Base

The database used in this study is the RAND Chronology of International

Terrorism for 1987, prepared by Gardela and Hoffman (1991). RAND is chosen over CIA data because it contains more than 5,500 chronological entries of international terrorism as far back as 1968. Scholars all over the world prefer the RAND data. The CIA data counts only official events. Therefore, RAND has a more predictive power for future terrorist events, occurrence of incidents, and the rate of victimization. Based on the Box-Jenkins approach (Box and Jenkins, 1970), RAND is more reliable and valid than the CIA data set. The Box-Jenkins method is based on a time-series analysis, which involves extracting the predictable changes from the observed data as obtained from "a series of progressive filters." The Box-Jenkins approach employs (in time-series) the three steps of analysis--identification, estimating, and forcasting.

Despite the Box-Jenkins potentials, terrorism is still difficult to study empirically because it involves numerous levels of political violence. Therefore, case studies have been employed by scholars to advance the knowledge of terrorism (Merkl, 1986). In this regard, chapter six will be based on the contextual analysis of terrorism in the WS. Case studies of the U.S., the U.S.S.R. and Cameroon will be studied as they relate to the core-periphery-semiperiphery WS structure.

The sources for the RAND Chronology are derived from more than 100 newspapers, journals, radio broadcasts, foreign press, and periodicals, surveyed mostly in English and five other languages. The sources are clipped, abstracted, coded, and entered into computer files. The RAND Chronology recognizes the ambiguity in the definition of terrorism. They prefer to define terrorism "as incidents in which terrorists go abroad to strike their targets, select victims or targets that have connections with foreign state (e.g., diplomats, foreign businessmen, offices of foreign corporations), or create international incidents by attacking airline passengers, personnel, and equipment" (Gardela and Hoffman, 1991:1).

Thus, terrorism is defined by the nature of the act and not by the identity of the perpetrators or their cause (i.e., RAND adheres to that type of terrorism designed to create an atmosphere of fear and alarm). From the definition, the use of violence or threat of violence is often directed against civilian targets. This means that terrorist aims are mostly political and are intended to produce effects beyond the immediate physical damage they cause. RAND's definition does not include domestic terrorism which are violent acts perpetrated by terrorists within their own country against their own nation. It also excludes state terrorism which is violence carried out by national governments against their own citizens.

Mickolus (1983) and Jenkins (1975, 1981) provided a detailed description of the RAND's definition and its operationalization.

Each terrorist event in the RAND database is characterized by coded variables such as date, type of action, type of target, geographical region, nationality of target and states at location. Among the tactics included in RAND's Chronology of International Terrorism are kidnapping; attack on installations; hijacking; bombing; barricade and hostage; assassination; and significant threat (i.e., actual incidents plus those that did not take place).

The total number of international terrorist incidents included in these data for 1987 numbered 394. These data demonstrate a continued decline in the level of international terrorism from 477 incidents in 1985 and 412 in 1986 (Gardela and Hoffman, 1991). RAND's 1987 data is the most recent and reliable (Cardela and Hoffman, 1991).

Conclusion

Basically, this chapter reviewed how different scholars have measured a country's position in the WS, the distribution of terrorism, and data used in the measurement of terrorism. Snyder and Kick's (1979) classifications with amendments (see table 4) are employed to measure a nation's location in the WS. Also the RAND's Chronology of International Terrorism for 1987 is the database which have been used by many scholars and which is found to be the most useful database for the purposes of this book. Like WS position, the measurement of terrorism has been difficult. Other sources of information on terrorist activity include the U.S. Central Intelligence Agency (CIA), and the U.S. Department of State. The CIA's documented trends on terrorism are based on an analysis of terrorist activity broken down by location, times, number of victims, type of action, and nationality of perpetrators and targets. The RAND Chronlology extends its breakdown of events to the type of tactics used by the terrorists. The next chapter will analyze the RAND Chronology for 1987 by placing countries in their respective WS regions and locations.

5. Analysis of the RAND Chronology of International Terrorism: 1987

Introduction

The aim of this chapter is to use tables to demonstrate how terrorism has occurred in different regions of the world. Countries in each region are allocated to their WS status based on WS locations noted in Table 4. The tables included in this section of the book shall consist of information on the countries where terrorism occurred, number of incidents, periphery, semiperiphery and core targets, and tactics used by the international terrorists. These tables will help to illustrate the regional distribution of international terrorist activity for 1987 and the WS positions of the countries mostly affected and targeted. Where possible, the 1986 record of international terrorism incidents based on Gardela and Hoffman (1987) study will be employed for comparison purposes.

Region A: Asia

The number of international terrorist activity in the region rose from forty-one incidents in 1986 to fifty-eight in 1987 (see Table 5: Breakdown of Incidents by Region for Asia in 1987). Overall, terrorism in Asia remained predominantly domestic in nature. Table 5 demonstrates that most terrorist incidents occurred in Pakistan and Philippines. There were 26 incidents in Pakistan and 21 in Philippines. Bombings were the preferred tactic used by terrorists. Twenty-three of the twenty-six terrorist incidents in Pakistan constituted indiscriminate bombings of diplomatic facilities, businesses, personnel, etc.

The New Peoples Army (NPA) and the military wing of Filipino

Communist Party mostly perpetrated the twenty-one international terrorist activities recorded for the Philippines. Together, they committed the majority (14) of the attacks. Seventy- percent (10) of these were against American business and military targets. NPA assassins popularly known as "sparrows" indiscriminately murdered two U.S. personnel and a U.S. retired Air Force officer (see incidents #308, #309, and #310 in the original 1987 RAND Chronology of International Terrorism). They also targeted Japanese industries resulting in the assassination of a Japanese journalist and the kidnapping of three Japanese business employees.

In the WS's status arrangement, twenty-five countries in the periphery were targeted, six in semiperiphery and twenty-seven in the core. The U.S. was the country most often targeted by terrorists in Asia in 1987. Indeed, eighteen of the attacks against core nations were directed against American citizens or interests followed by four attacks on Japanese interests. The U.S. was mostly attacked in the Philippines, which accounted for thirteen terrorist incidents against the U.S. and its interests. Why then has the U.S. been targeted more often than any other nation by the Asian terrorists? In fact, this book will endeavor to provide some answers to this question.

Region B: Europe

In Europe the number of international terrorist incidents in 1987 declined somewhat from that of 1986--from 123 to 97 (see Table 6: Breakdown of Incidents by Region for Europe in 1987). However, the number of terrorist incidents in most European countries remained virtually the same. For instance, Spain in 1987 recorded 28 international terrorist incidents compared to 29 in 1986; Greece experienced 10 in 1986 and 12 in 1937, whereas Italy had 6 in 1986 and 4 incidents in 1987. Britain and France were exceptions to this pattern. Britain had 11 international terrorist incidents in 1987 while it only experienced 5 incidents in 1986. On the other hand, France dropped from 40 in 1986 to 15 in 1987. Table 6 shows that most incidents occurred in Spain, followed by France and Federal Republic of Germany (FRG).

There were a total of 69 incidents against core nations, 16 incidents were perpetrated against semiperiphery nations, and only 12 attacks were against periphery countries. Various Middle Eastern émigré groups such as Iranians, Kurds, members of the Palestinian Popular Front, and Lebanese citizens carried out most of the international terrorist incidents in Europe in 1987. However, terrorism by European domestic terrorist groups remained a major concern. Again as in Asia, the U.S. was the core nation mostly targeted by terrorist attacks accounting for 26 incidents. Other core targets including France experienced 15 attacks, and Britain experienced 12 incidents against its citizens and interests. The U.S. citizens and interests were mostly targeted in Spain where 13 incidents in the form of bombings and attacks were perpetrated.

Region C: Latin America

In 1987, 98 international terrorist incidents occurred in Latin America while 110 terrorist incidents were recorded in 1986 (Gardela and Hoffman, 1991). As a venue for international incidents, Latin America ranked second falling behind the Middle East. As in other regions, international terrorism against U.S. targets make up the highest portion of terrorist events in Latin America in 1987. Most terrorism in Latin America is related to local insurgencies. Table 7 (Breakdown of Incidents by Region for Latin America in 1987) demonstrated that Peru, Colombia and Chile accounted for the majority of the Latin American international terrorist activity.

However, fewer incidents were recorded for Peru in 1987 which had only 38 incidents compared with 47 in 1986, and Colombia's 13 in 1987 versus 30 in 1986. In Chile, where the government sponsors terrorism (U.S. Department of State, 1988) the number of incidents remained the same (14 incidents for both years). Of the 98 Latin American terrorist incidents recorded in 1987, 78 were targeted against the core nations of the world. Thirteen of the incidents targeted peripheral nations while only 5 incidents were directed against semiperipheral societies. In Chile and Colombia, where terrorism occurred 14 and 13 times respectively, the U.S. alone was targeted 11 times each in both cases. In Peru, where 38 incidents occurred, a large proportion (21 incidents) was directed against the U.S. In short, as in other regions, the U.S. was the preferred target for international terrorists using a variety of tactics (such as kidnapping, bombing, and assassination) against U.S. citizens and interests.

Region D: Middle East

The Middle East experienced the highest number of international terrorist incidents in 1987, recording 113 (versus 122 in 1986, see Table 8: Breakdown of Incidents by Region for Middle East in 1987). The two major terrorist organizations were Palestinian and Shi'a terrorist groups who claimed responsibility for two-thirds of the attacks in 1987. The remainder of the incidents listed in RAND were committed by Iraqi, Iranian, Syrian, Kurdish, Turkish, Libyan, Lebanese, Sudanese, Egyptian, and Moroccan terrorist organizations perpetrating acts of violence in the region (see Table 8).

Table 8 illustrates that 41 international terrorist incidents occurred in Lebanon (considered a semiperipheral country by Snyder and Kick), which means that Lebanon witnessed the highest number of international terrorist events in the Middle East in 1987. Israel also ranked as a semiperipheral nation, and a close ally of the U.S. recorded 35 incidents, while Turkey came a distant third with only 7 incidents. In this region core nations were targeted 45 times compared to a close 40 attacks against semiperipheral nations, whereas peripheral countries were targeted 26 times. The state of Israel was the country mostly targeted in the Middle East with a total of 32 attacks while the U.S. ranked second with 14 international terrorist incidents against U.S. citizens and interests. A majority of the attacks against Israel took place in the nation of Israel itself and were mostly perpetrated by Palestinian terrorists (Gardela and Hoffman, 1991). The terrorists used a combination of tactics such as kidnapping, bombing, assassinations, and attacks to achieve their terrorist goals.

Region E: North America

North America has been recognized as a region with the least international terrorist activities. In 1987, the North American region also experienced the fewest international incidents among all the regions studied by the RAND Chronology of International Terrorism (Gardela and Hoffman, 1991). Table 9 (Breakdown of Incidents by Region for North America in 1987) indicates that only eight international incidents occurred in the North American region in 1987 compared with seven incidents in 1986. All of these incidents took place in the United States. Although these events took place in the U.S., only two incidents were targeted against the U.S. (a core nation), three incidents were against India, USSR and Cuban interests (all semi-peripheral nations), while three incidents were targeted against peripheral nations (two against El Salvador and one against Vietnamese interests).

Like in Europe, ethnic or émigré terrorist groups perpetrated most international terrorist incidents in the U.S. Most of their complaints have no relevance to internal American policies; rather they regard America as the buffer zone where international battles are fought (Gardela and Hoffman, 1991). A review of the RAND Chronology demonstrates that except for the hijacking of Alaskan Airlines passenger jets (incident #057) the remaining seven incidents recorded were conducted by ethnic or émigré groups. These include Anti-Castro Cuban exiles (incident #147); radical Sikh nationalists (incident #152); Jewish Militants with a close affiliation with the Jewish Defense League's east coast chapter (incident #192); Committee to Exterminate the Communists and Restore the Nation in California (incident #248); and Salvadoran death squads operating in the United States (incident #216). Although, the U.S. is the core nation mostly targeted by terrorists, fewer terrorist activities actually take place in the U.S. This may be due to the fact that the U.S. has a strong antiterrorism program. The U.S. also protects its boarders and possesses the modern technology that makes a proactive strategy to combat terrorism on U.S. soil a reality.

Region F: Sub-Saharan Africa/West Africa

The RAND Chronology of International Terrorism did not list any incidents in the Republic of South Africa or any of the West African nations. This may be due to the definition of terrorism RAND prefers in its recording of terrorism around the globe.

Table 10 (Breakdown of Incidents by Region in Sub-Saharan Africa for 1987) shows that no international terrorist events occurred in either South Africa or any of the West African nations such as Nigeria. Historically, Sub-Saharan African nations have experienced low levels of international terrorism. Recently Kenya and Tanzania experienced terrorist activities that claimed many lives. When such incidents occur in Sub-Saharan Africa, like a rebel attack on a missionary station in Zimbabwe, where 16 innocent church workers and members of their families were murdered, they receive less publicity by the international press (see incident #358). It may be due to the fact that the international press does not pay attention to isolated events in Africa. These terrorists events where innocent people are slaughtered mercilessly are no less tragic than the terrorist attacks that take place on London and Paris streets.

Another reason for the absence of terrorism in Africa may be the reality that less terrorism occurs in this region of the world. As table 10 illustrates, only 18 incidents were recorded in this region for 1987 compared to 7 in 1986. Compared to other regions, most incidents were perpetrated by different guerrilla armies or national liberation movements. In this part of the region, states are interested in sponsoring terrorism (incident #068). The popular tactics used in this region are kidnappings (seven), followed by assassination, which is the common tactic employed by the state-sponsored incidents such as the murder of three African National Congress Officials (incidents #169, #213, and #287).

Finally of all terrorist incidents in this region, a total of 9 incidents were targeted against the core, 2 against the semiperiphery, and 5 incidents against peripheral nations. What follows is an additional analysis of tables to demonstrate that terrorists more often target core nations than semiperiphery and periphery nations.

Terrorism and World System Position

The goal of this section is to show that core nations are targeted by international terrorists more than any other countries in the world. Table 11 groups terrorist incidents by WS position of country of occurrence and WS position of target. Other tables contain a chronological classification of the RAND's International Chronology of terrorist activities that occurred in 1987.

Table 11 illustrates how terrorism is distributed in the WS. The argument that the structural nature of colonialism, imperialism, and neocolonialism results in terrorist acts of violence against core nations or colonizers tend to be supported by this table. The colonized peripheral nations use terrorism against the imperial countries to express the oppressive economic and political set backs of their countries. Since these countries have no economic and political power, they accept the use of structural violence in order to receive attention from the militarily, economically, and politically diversified core countries.

Table 11 demonstrates that 13 core countries were targeted 233 times in separate terrorism incidents in 1987, while 44 peripheral nations were targeted for a total of 136 times. In 167 of the 233 terrorist incidents targeting core nations, the attack occurred in a peripheral nation. In comparison, terrorists targeted peripheral nations only 16 times within the borders of core nations. The purpose of such attacks appears to be to gain publicity and to draw core nation's attention to problems in peripheral nations.

It can be deduced from this table and others that follow that structural terrorism exacted against peripheral countries is direct. It consists of the domination-dependency syndrome created by imperialism in its numerous cultural, economic, political, scientific, technological and other forms. Imperialism sponsors petty and comparodor bourgeoisie in peripheral and (even semiperipheral) countries which results in national economic dependence and humiliating poverty of the masses. This structural creation of inequality may lead to suppression of the masses, which creates repressive governments. The resultant consequence may be international terrorism to gain the attention of the powerful core nations such as the United States of America and the United Kingdom.

Due to the American position in the political and economic life of the world, and due to its powerful influence as the only acclaimed super power, repressive groups in a peripheral nation look at the United States as the only hope by exacting violence on interests or areas that might receive consideration by the core areas of the world. In fact, in table 11, the 64 terrorists incidents that were targeted against the core in the core areas were not perpetrated by core countries themselves. Most of these incidents were still the work of dissatisfied groups sympathizing with one peripheral nation or the other. Could one imagine a United Kingdom government sponsoring terrorism incidents against the United States and vice versa? Some émigré groups were responsible for most of the attacks that occurred in core nations. Most importantly, state governments sponsored most of the incidents.

Discussion

Although international terrorism incidents still constitute a menace to the modern WS, the degree of terrorist incidents declined from 412 in 1986 to 394 in 1987. International terrorists were more lethal than active in 1987.

The total number of human beings fatally slaughtered in 1987 by terrorists amounted to 374 compared with 329 in 1986. There was a dramatic increase of 11 percent in the number of people murdered in 1987 against the fatalities recorded in 1986.

In the regions studied, Europe, the Middle East, and Latin America continued to account for most of the world's recorded terrorist incidents (78 percent). However, the Middle East tops the rest of the regions in the total number of incidents recorded (see Table 12 for a hierarchical breakdown). Among the countries in the WS, the United States (a core nation) was the country most frequently targeted by terrorists with a total number of 121 attacks on U.S. citizens or interests. Israel (35), France (25), United Kingdom (22) and Pakistan (20) follow the U.S. (see Table 13: Five Nationalities most often targeted by international terrorists for 1987). However, the U.S. was not among the top ten nationalities with the most terrorist events as recorded in Table 14: (Ten Nationalities with the Most International Terrorist Incidents for 1987). Lebanon surpassed every other nation in the number of terrorist occurrences in a particular country in 1987, followed by Peru, Israel, Spain, Pakistan, Philippines, France, Chile, Colombia, and Federal Republic of Germany (Gardela and Hoffman, 1991).

A cross-classification (Table 15) of tactics and regions indicates that bombings were the preferred method employed by peripheral terrorists in 1987 accounting for 50 percent of all terrorist acts, resembling a pattern unchanged in more than twenty years (Gardela and Hoffman, 1991). Terrorists prefer to use bombs because it draws enormous attention (i.e., core attention) to their causes and to plant a bomb requires less organizational expertise and logistics needed in more sophisticated tactics such as kidnapping, and assassinations against protected targets (Gardela and Hoffman, 1991).

Bombings are followed in ranking by attacks on installations (25 percent), kidnapping (13 percent), and assassination/ shooting (13 percent, while other tactics such as hijacking and hostage situations accounted for only 5 percent in terms of target and region (See Table 16: Cross-descriptions of Target and Region). Business and diplomatic targets shared the number one and two positions in the level of the frequency of attacks. Businesses were attacked in 27 percent of all international terrorist incidents recorded, while 20 percent of events were against diplomatic targets. But civilians were targeted 11 percent as evidenced in the RAND Chronology of International Terrorism. It may be deduced that terrorists are directing assaults on innocent citizens more frequently. They have come to regard civilians as important elements of a successful terrorist attack. Terrorist acts of violence have become more indiscriminate with increasing frequency of assaults against civilians who happen to be in the wrong place at the wrong time (Gardela and Hoffman, 1991). Perhaps, wherever possible, terrorists have elected to murder citizens suspected to be of U.S. origin or other members of the core nations for publicity purposes. They do this in order to-solicit the attention of the world for the benefit of their violent ideological causes.

Conclusion

The use of the RAND Chronology of International Terrorism in this book suggests that West African nations have not participated in international terrorist activities. The RAND Chronology did not record any incidents at all for these countries, and this may be attributed to the resilience of traditions inherent in these societies. Moreover, international terrorists may not prefer to operate in these nations due to the fact that the global press has an attitude of indifference when it comes to Africa. This position is dramatically changing with recent events in Africa discussed in chapter seven.

Tables were employed to demonstrate the distribution of terrorism in different regions of the world according to incidents, countries of occurrence, tactics, and periphery, semiperiphery, and core targets of international terrorism for 1987. The findings suggest that international terrorist acts are targeted against core nations when compared to terrorist acts directed against peripheral and semiperipheral nations. Even when a semiperipheral nation (e.g., Israel) is targeted, evidence demonstrates that it has a close tie with a core nation (e.g., U.S.).

6. Labeling Terrorism in Context

Introduction

The goal of this chapter is to examine how a WS position of power determines the definition of terrorism. Three countries, the U.S., USSR, and Cameroon are used as case studies. Each represents a different WS position. Finally, suggestion will be provided on the need for a paradigm shift in the study of terrorism within criminology.

As argued in chapter two, the labeling of an act as a terrorist act in the WS depends on who has the power to do the defining. Terrorism, like crime or any other phenomenon is a social creation. Those who command power over others will not hesitate to label an act a terrorist act when that behavior is contrary to the interests of those who wield great power. The word terrorism, therefore, is socially constructed. It may have different meaning in Cameroon, the U.S., or the former Soviet Union (Russia) depending on the context of its occurrence.

Behaviors are not inherently terroristic. In criminology, murder, rape, assault, fraud, etc., are not necessarily crimes until they are officially defined and reacted to as crime. Terrorism, like these vicious crimes are injurious to the members of society, but an act is not a terrorist act until it has been labeled. It can be posited, according to labeling theorists (Becker, 1963; Erickson, 1966; Tannenbaum, 1938; Lemert, 1951) "that what makes an act criminal is not the harm it incurs but whether this label is conferred upon the act by the state" (Lilly, et al, 1989). It means that a state has the power to label any behavior injurious to society as a terrorist act regardless of the location of that state in the WS power distribution. It is the pattern of a nation's reaction to an event and the reality it constructs not necessarily the type of behavior exhibited that makes an act a terrorist act. The role of power in the social construction of terrorism is essential and shall be examined more fully below.

"Power and Anti-Powerism"

Jones (1987) argued that oppression, historically, engenders resistance. Such resistance may be armed resistance. According to Jones (1987: 202):

> Historically speaking, oppression is initiated through the violence of the oppressor. The pattern that history reveals is this: there is an original violence that initiates and establishes the economic social and political inequalities that comprise oppression. With the establishment of a relation of oppression, violence has already begun. However, the oppressor invariably suffers historical amnesia regarding this original violence, or that violence is transmitted into a more benign action through the oppressors' power to legitimate.

The exploitation, alienation, and powerlessness they have been forced to accept motivate the oppressed terrorists. They are encouraged not to seek power but to resent it. The predator prefers the prey to be anti-power. "Anti-powerism regards power as essentially negative or evil" (Jones, 1987). The tactic of oppression is to compel the oppressed to accept the "philosophy of antipowerism." Powerism, readily accepts power since it is essential in the maintenance of oppression. In Jones (1987: 203) assessment, "power, from this perspective, is neutral neither evil nor good; rather its quality depends upon who wields it and for what purpose." Power is used by the powerful to legitimate its actions such as terrorism as moral and right.

Oppressors, like in the former Republic of South Africa (RSA), legitimate its reign whenever it uses terrorism against the oppressed majority population. The RSA by abusing its exercise of executive power claims national security interests to justify its illegitimate actions. Herman (1987) demonstrated the role of power in the definition and labeling of terrorism. Those who have power selects what acts constitute terrorism. Herman (1984:1) states:

> The powerful naturally define terrorism to exclude their own acts and those of their friends and clients.

In 1985, as I have already alluded to in chapter two, President Reagan labeled North Korea, Libya, Iran, Cuba, and Nicaragua as terrorist states. Omitted in that list were RSA, Israel, and Guatemala (Herman, 1987). In order to comprehend how the powerful label the behaviors of the enemy and friendly states, one has to study terrorism contextually. Archbishop Camera (Jones, 1987) demonstrated that violence has three indivisible dimensions. Jones (1987) labeled the first dimension as original violence or institutionalized or structural violence. The second tier is counter-violence while the third tier is repressive violence. Below, these dimensions will be discussed and applied contextually in the WS's definition of terrorism.

The Three Dimensions of Terrorism

Institutionalized violence is that type of violence that establishes and lays the groundwork for oppression. It engenders violence and maintains the system of oppression (Jones, 1987). To illustrate, the majority of the acts of terrorism/violence that occur in South Africa are the direct result of institutionalized terrorism by the minority regime. Violence in South Africa is caused not by the African National Congress, but by the minority regime's security forces.

In Carmara's phenomenology of violence, counter violence (Jones, 1987) is the result of institutionalized violence. This is the violence used by the oppressed to counter the devastating effects of the institutionalized violence. In other words, this is the violence employed by the African National Congress or the Palestinian Liberation Organization (PLO) forces against their oppressors. Finally, counter violence triggers repressive violence used by those who wield power. Authorities to quell the actions of the "practitioners" of counter violence use repressive violence. This also activates counter violence and the cycle of terrorism emerges again until all parties accept non-violence (Jones, 1987; Newman and Lynch, 1988).

These three dimensions of violence (terrorism and their meanings) depend again on who has the power to label those acts that fall within the three tiers. "Moreover, this political and contextual nature of violence means that the definition of violence itself is always an exercise in power" (Jones, 1987: 206).

For example, what counter violence meant in Carmaral's contextual analysis might be different in today's construction of terrorism. Because the powerful use different semantics in their labeling of terrorism, counter terrorism in contemporary study of terrorism is referred to as that type of terror used by the state for a long period of time to destabilize the opposition (Herman, 1987). In addition to counter terrorism, powerful states also use the semantic of retaliation to represent a response to an immediate preceding act (Herman, 1987). This makes it necessary to develop another language; that of counterterror which permits "a more continuous assault on the basis and populations of terrorists" (Herman, 1987). In short, the powerful and their friends use retaliation for immediate violent responses and counterterror for longer-term attacks.

To illustrate, the rigid apartheid RSA's constant use of terrorism against its neighbors to dissuade them from accommodating the ANC and SWAPO "terrorists" is, in the powerful semantics usage, counterterrorism. Also, the brutal massacre of peasants by the Guatemalan government to wipe out any strong political opposition (i.e., terrorists) is identically labeled counterterror in the eyes of those who control power. Herman concluded, that counterterror is nothing but a "dressed up form of state (wholesale) terror." The point is that the allies of powerful nations in the WS are seen as using retaliation or counterterrorism. These states are never viewed by other friendly core nations as employing terrorism, regardless of the action (i.e., the massacre of blacks in South Africa or Palestinian groups in the Middle East). At the same time, Herman argued that the enemies of the powerful nations (e.g., PLO and ANC) are not viewed as using retaliation when they engage in terrorism. Powerless nations are typically labeled as the terrorists, the aggressors, and never as the nations or groups that are wronged.

The context in which terrorism is defined as seen from Jones (1987) and Herman (1987) perspectives provide us the opportunity to look at situations in which the core, periphery and semiperiphery nations have responded to other nations' acts or actions within a particular state as terrorist acts. In short, the subject of the case studies that follow is to see how nations label activities as terrorism.

Case Studies of the Labeling of Terrorism in the World System

Core Nation: U.S.A.

The goal of this section is to demonstrate how the U.S. has labeled acts of terrorism in three nations--Nicaragua, Israel and South Africa. Between 1911 and 1933, the U.S. Marines occupied Nicaragua. When the Marines left in 1933, Anastasio Somoza seized the presidency (Carl, 1987). For 43 years, Somoza and his family, with the help of the U.S., governed Nicaragua repressively (Carl, 1987; Pfost, 1987). In 1979, a revolutionary movement emerged, and the Sandinista National Liberation Front (FSLN), overthrew the Somoza regime (Pfost, 1987; Walker, 1982).

As soon as the Sandinistas assumed power, they established different basic programs that would improve the quality of life of the Nicaraguan people (Pfost, 1987). These include the Literacy Crusade, basic changes in health care clinics such as reducing malaria and vaccination of one million children against polio, measles, and tetanus. The Sandinistas also embarked on agricultural reforms aimed at food production. The reforms earned Sandinistas the UNESCO Literacy Prize in 1980 (Pfost, 1987; Brandt, 1980) and the 1982 UNICEF World Health Organization Prize (Pfost, 1987).

Shortly after the Reagan administration began, it designed policies aimed at overthrowing the Nicaraguan government (see Pfost, 1987, for chronology of events). Such policies led to the establishment of the Contra opposition to the Nicaraguan regime. Pfost (1987) noted that by 1984 the contra war resulted in over 7,000 casualties, including murders and injuries of children. About 1,019 Sandinista soldiers died while over 1,798 were injured.

In a study conducted by Brody (1985: 21-22) Contra terrorism included:

> Attacks on purely civilian targets resulting in the killing of unarmed men, women, children, and the elderly. Premeditated acts of brutality including rape, beatings, mutilation, and torture; Individual and mass kidnappings of civilians, particularly in the Northern Atlantic coast region for the purpose of forced recruitment into the Contra forces and the creation of a hostage refugee population in Honduras; Assaults on economic and social targets such as farms, cooperatives, food storage facilities, and health centers, including a particular effort to disrupt the coffee harvests through attacks on coffee cooperatives and on vehicles carrying volunteer coffee

harvesters; Intimidation of civilians who participate or cooperate in government or community programs, such as distribution of subsidized food products, rural cooperatives, education and the local self-defense militia; and kidnapping, intimidation, and even murder of religious leaders who support the government, including priests and clergy-trained lay pastors.

The Sandinistas themselves have been accused of committing most of the atrocities of which the Contras are accused. Adolfo, et al, (1985) argued that the Sandinistas became an instrument of foreign interests and maintained a totalitarian control of Nicaragua. They argued that the Contras would restore a democratic system in place of the communism and socialism preferred by the Sandinistas. In the words of these authors, the Contras were fighting for pluralism and freedom and the protection of human rights for all Nicaraguans.

Using this brief description of the situation in Nicaragua, we can now address the question: how then has terrorism been labeled in such a situation? In the WS's arrangement, the U.S. as a core nation has the power to define in such a case the groups that were using acts of terrorism. According to President Reagan's speech delivered to the American people March 16, 1986 (Quoted in Adolfo, et al. 1985), the Contras are freedom fighters not terrorists. Reagan put it in the following manner:

> When the Sandinistas betrayed the revolution, many who had fought the old Somoza dictatorship literally took to the hills, and like the French Resistance that fought the Nazis, began fighting the Soviet block communists and the Nicaraguan collaborators. These few have now been joined by thousands with their blood and courage, the freedom fighters of Nicaragua have pinned down the Sandinista Army and bought the people of Central America precious time. We Americans owe them a debt of gratitude. In helping to thwart the Sandinistas and their Soviet Mentors, the resistance has contributed directly to the security of the United States.

This means that the U.S. government labeled the Contras as freedom fighters, whose objective was to eliminate communism and usher in a democratic system in Nicaragua. This situation is, in theory, in the best interest of the U.S. because of the national security issues involved (Chamorro, 1985). In the WS's definition of terrorism, the Nicaraguan government is a terrorist state, even though, many Latin American countries argued that the Contras are terrorists who brutally murdered and injured defenseless civilians in their desire to overthrow the legitimate Sandinistan government (Chamarro, 1985). But in order to fully understand how power plays a role in the labeling of terrorism, other case studies are necessary for full comprehension. Let us then see how the U.S. has labeled terrorism when it comes to the "Palestinian Question" and the state of Israel.

In Israel the main conflict between Palestinians and Israel is land. By the United Nations mandate, the Jewish people were allowed to occupy or own the land previously named Palestine. This arrangement caused many Palestinians to reside in other Arab nations forfeiting the homeland they have occupied for centuries. However, millions of Palestinians still live in Israel (Moughrabi, 1992). To control the Palestinians who reside in the occupied West Bank and Gaza strip, Israel has denied legal citizenship to Palestinians and has used forced evictions against the Palestinian population. This delicate situation results in terrorism as evidenced in many bloody, tragic battles between Israelis and Arab nationalists and has given rise to what is popularly known as the "Palestinian Question" (Moughrabi, 1992).

Moughrabi (1992:46) reported that in response to the Israeli occupation, the Palestinians used different tactics of resistance aimed to abolish Israel's occupation and regain self-rule over their land. The Palestinians organized a national uprising (intifida) in 1987, which led to the death of many of them. In 1991, the Israeli officials murdered 962 Palestinians, 252 of those killed were 16 years old or younger. About 115,118 people have been injured, 66 activists have been subjected to deportation (recently about 400 were deported), while 15,100 Palestinians are under house arrest. The official mouthpiece of the Palestinians is the Palestinian Liberation organization (PLO).

Despite overwhelming power, Israel has not succeeded in ending Palestinian opposition (Moughrabi, 1992). Israel adopted different strategies to stop the Palestinian uprising. These include the use of massive force designed to make the Palestinians live a life of fear. The reason for the use of excessive force is the "delegitimation of the Palestinian Arabs among Israelis. In short, the Israelis look at Arabs as subhuman, two-legged beasts, drugged cockroaches, grasshoppers, demons, or bloodthirsty devils" (Moughrabi, 1992). Palestinians are also described as violence prone, deviates, parasites, and psychopaths who can only understand the language of force (Benzinan, 1989).   Finally, Israel uses "political policing" to control the behavior of the Palestinians, and has embarked on controlling the infrastructure of the whole occupied territories.   The goal is to establish a Jewish permanent settlement.

Land is the primary bone of contention between the two parties. Moughrabi (1991: 50) described it as follows:

> Another key factor is the centrality of the land issue.   In Palestine, there was no free land; it was settled for thousands of years by a stable peasant society.   For Zionist settlers, control of the land was crucial for the establishment of a state.   For the Palestinian natives, control of the land became synonymous with the control of their own destiny.   Zionist settlers initially bought some of the land, but after 1947, they took it over by conquest.   In the West Bank and Gaza Strip, more than half the total land area has been confiscated to establish Jewish colonies.

This same situation existed in the RSA where the majority blacks were constantly murdered, and in North America where the Native Indians were exterminated.   In these two contexts as in Israel, terrorism played a significant part in subduing the original occupants of the land.   In the WS's arrangement, the U.S., a core powerful nation, prefers to define terrorism as violence directed against governments.   By excluding friendly states as terrorist actors, Israel and South Africa are removed from the terrorist list. This means that the ANC and the PLO cannot escape the definition and are automatically labeled as terrorist organizations (Herman, 1987).   Ironically there is a double standard here that should be noted.   As reviewed earlier, the Nicaraguan government qualified as a terrorist state in the eyes of President Reagan and his intellectual spokespersons.   This ability to define and redefine who is a terrorist is available only to the powerful core nations.

But why have Israel and RSA been protected from the terrorist label?   Herman (1987) argued that the states protected from the terrorism label are allies and clients of the U.S. or other core nations, while the groups labeled terrorists oppose these allies and the core's protection of the status quo.   Pieterse (1987: 203) stated, "the most common explanation is that Israel is a strategic asset to the United states in the Middle East--a very expensive but unsinkable extension of the U.S. Sixth Fleet."   The influence of the Jewish lobby in the United States is also often mentioned.   Israel also plays a vital role in the United States policy to expand in the Middle East and other parts of the world by providing essential assistance to its core ally.

The same argument can be made about South Africa because of its economic and strategic importance to the United States. The U.S. is dependent on foreign sources of supply for many of the raw materials essential for its defense and economy. For example, 86 percent of the world's platinum reserves is in South Africa, including 53 percent of the world's manganese, 64 percent of vanadium, 95 percent of chromium, 52 percent of cobalt. In addition, diamonds, coal, gold, uranium, copper and other critical minerals are produced in South Africa (Lisker, 1986). The importance of these minerals justifies the labeling of the ANC as a communist or terrorist organization since the former Soviet Union had penetrated the organization as the opposition claimed. It is then critical to legitimize the racist, rigid, apartheid regime, and avoid labeling it a terrorist state. In short, the ANC is a terrorist and communist organization since the Soviet Union provides support for it. Lisker (1986: 96) puts it as follows:

> Founded in 1912 as a purely black nationalist movement with its prime objectives the securing of political rights for the black majority (ANC) has become . . . a front organization for the South African communist party. With the full support of the Soviet Union and its allies, it has resorted to terrorism in order to achieve its political ends.

This research is opposed to the writings of those who tend to lend legitimacy to South Africa's racist tyranny by undermining the liberation of black Africans. Painting the ANC as terrorists and communists shifts world opinion against African Liberation efforts in favor of apartheid. The South African government practiced terrorism. What the ANC did and the PLO are doing are not different from what Contras did in Nicaragua. In fact, Africans in South Africa fought for their father's land, which constituted an essential part of their quality of life. Core powers should realize that when you denied a people their right to land you have deliberately denied them their livelihood. The PLO must also realize that Israel has an inalienable right to exist regardless of Arab opposition. The next section examines how the Soviet Union, a semiperipheral nation labels terrorism within the Soviet society and externally.

Semiperipheral Nation: U.S.S.R.

In this section, the issue is to examine situations in which the former Soviet Union labeled acts of terrorism outside the Soviet hemisphere. The difficulty lies in the principle that the Soviet Union (Russia) does not deny its friendship and support with revolutionary groups, but it rejects the labeling of revolutionary methods as "terrorists" (Schagheck, 1990; Poland, 1988; Golan, 1990; Elad and Merari, 1984). As a result, Soviet policies toward terrorism have never been clear (Golan, 1990). Russian attitudes and messages to groups such as the PLO and the ANC has centered on the abandonment of armed struggle (terrorism), and to seek political solutions to problems (Golan, 1990).

However, Francis (1986) argued that the Soviets support international terrorism in order to achieve their goals, the overthrow of the United States. The author contended that considerable evidence exist to show that Russia is actively engaged in the support of terrorism, guerrilla warfare, and insurgency movements. This is accomplished through satellites or surrogates. A satellite includes a government, country, or organization that is controlled by Moscow. Examples of Satellite nations and groups are Cuba, East Germany, Czechoslovakia, or the World Peace Organization. A surrogate, on the other hand, is a government, country, or organization that acts as a substitute for the Russians. These include the PLO, Libya, North Korea, Iran, and Syria. These two terms can be used interchangeably. The obvious difference is that a surrogate government, country, or organization such as Libya and the PLO do not subscribe to the orthodox Marxist-Leninist ideology. Surrogates, however, receive assistance from Moscow and its satellites. According to Francis (1986) "a surrogate can be a satellite, but it is not necessarily one." The advantage of using surrogates for Moscow is to distance itself from embarrassing policies. Surrogates are therefore used to train and support nations and organizations that participate in international terrorism.

Herman (1983) disagreed with the above analysis. He contended that it is absurd to place the blame for the increase of worldwide terrorism on Moscow. He asserted that Soviet surrogates or satellites are propaganda. For example, Herman argued that Kaddafi was not elevated to power by significant Soviet assistance. Russia does not control what Libya does.

But regardless of the academic disagreements and semantics, the fact remains that the Soviet Union, like the U.S., has the power to label acts of terrorism. In contrast to the U.S., the Soviet Union has referred to Israel and South Africa as terrorist states. Included in its non-terrorist list are Contras, China and Iran (Poland, 1988; Golan, 1990). Clearly, in the WS power arrangement, the U.S. has the upper hand in determining what constitutes terrorism, and that is why its definition, rather than the Soviet Union, is more broadly accepted.

Soviet policy makers prefer to use the terms "resistance or guerrilla warfare" when they are supporting a particular movement or classify the same acts as terrorism during periods of non-support. This is true with the Eritreans, the Kurds of Iraq, the Tamils of India, the PLO and the Turkish terrorists. Whatever may be the case, labeling of terrorism depends on the Soviet's interest just as has been discussed with the U.S..

Soviet labeling of terrorism depends on its military and political objectives. Although, as a socialist nation, it rejects imperialism, its actions in Afghanistan have imperialist undertones. Soviet objectives or interests include the desire to destabilize the Western democracies; expansion of Moscow influence throughout the WS; and to support pro-Russian freedom movements to gain power. More practical goals consist of the utilization of terrorism to subdue groups and regimes that are anti-communism, and to instigate the free world to overreact (Poland, 1988). Soviet involvement in Afghanistan is the best situation to illustrate Russian pattern of the labeling of terrorism in the global society.

The Soviet Union, in 1979, was requested by the Afghan government to help quell resistance movements. Moscow entered Afghanistan with full force. They invaded with tanks and soldiers. The Soviet arsenal included chemical weapons, toy bombs, rape, and destabilization of Afghan agriculture (Wheeler, 1986). Wheeler (1986) argued that the Afghan Mujaheddin were "holy warriors" whose objective was to defeat an evil, heartless regime. Wheeler labeled the Afghan Mujaheddin as freedom fighters. The Soviets, in Wheeler's view, committed atrocities against the Afghan citizenry.

Wheeler contended that the Soviet Union policy in Afghanistan was to murder and terrorize innocent people including women and children. The Kremlin's atrocities in Afghanistan led to the extermination of over 100,000 Mujaheddin. The number of women and children killed were more than 800,000. In Wheeler's analysis, this systematic campaign of butchery is a deliberate act of terrorism. Others have argued that Moscow's occupation of Afghanistan was purely a humanitarian mission, since the Mujaheddin leaders engaged in sabotage and terror against the "peoples government" (Ustinov, 1986). Ustinov (1986: 170-171) writes:

> Their (Mugaheddin) main objective is to frighten the population and provoke unrest. Terrorist acts are carried out by groups specially trained for the purpose by experts from the secret services of the U.S., Pakistan and a number of West European countries. They kill and kidnap party and government officials and servicemen, conduct acts of sabotage in public places, at airports, fuel storages, pump houses, electric power stations and on transport, and shell housing estates from mobile guns, mortars and other weapons.

From the forgoing, it is obvious that Moscow regarded the Afghan rebels or holy warriors as terrorists. However, the Kremlin preferred to name Mujaheddin forces as counter revolutionaries who used sabotage and terror tactics to cripple the Afghan "peoples' government." The U.S. regarded the Afghan holy warriors as freedom fighters, whereas, the USSR did not see anything terroristic in the actions of the Afghan's government.

So far, it has been demonstrated that both the core and the semiperiphery nations label acts as terrorism depending on who is acting or who is defining. Herman (1987) argued that terror is what the powerful declares to be terror and since they take the word loosely they take the attitude of "if I don't like it, call it terrorism" definition of terrorism. What remains to be seen is how and what conditions peripheral nations define and label acts of terrorism. Do they have the same interests as the core and the semiperiphery?

Periphery Nation: Cameroon

The rise of terrorism in Cameroon has been attributed to the activities of the former nationalist party, the Union des Populations du Cameroun (UPC). The United Republic of Cameroon, known as the "hinge of Africa," is located in the Western part of the continent. Cameroon was a German colony until World War I when imperial Germany was defeated. Cameroon was then divided into a western section under British control, and an eastern section under French administration. The UPC was organized in French Cameroon in 1948 with the help of trade unionists and state employees. Its objective as a nationalist party was full independence and the reunification of the Cameroons (Uku-Wertimer, 1988; Levine, 1971; Denmark and Welfling, 1988).

In February 1961, the British imperial government held a plebiscite in British Cameroon, under UN's supervision. The goal was to determine whether British Cameroonians wished to be joined with Nigeria or remain a part of the new Republic of Cameroon. Despite political oppositions and tensions, the northern area voted to form a union with Nigeria. However, on October 1, 1961, reunification of Cameroon was realized (Levine, 1971).

Earlier, French hostility led to the use of violent tactics by UPC in 1955. The UPC was subsequently banned. The UPC then splintered into two violent political factions. Nyobe and Matip led one group and Moumie, Quandie and Kingue led the other faction. Throughout the colonial period the UPC continued its rebellious activities against the colonial administrators. In 1960, when Cameroon regained her independence as one country, government leadership rested with Ahidjo and his Union Camerounaise (UC) party. At this Juncture, the UPC wing of Nyobe and Matip, which remained in the country was legalized while the wing headed by Moumie and his group remained in exile and continued its violent opposition (Levine, 1971; Denmark and Welfling, 1988). In short, from 1955 until the mid-1960s Cameroon was confronted by continuous terrorist activity led by the Outlawed UPC group and supported by foreign communist and radical African regimes (Mongo, 1964).

Although ethnic imbalance was a significant source of conflict and tension, political repression was the major basis for continued opposition. President Ahidjo consolidated all political parties and established only one political party. The UC (Union Cametounaise) then as a single state party was able to co-opt opposition members, and where it failed, used drastic measures such as arrest and detention of political opponents (Levine, 1971).

By the early 1970s, the Ahidjo government kept a large number of political prisoners most of which were associated with the UPC rebellion (Legun, 1975). The situation continued into the 1980s. The UPC in exile remained the only viable opposition to the one-party system. It refused reconciliation with the Ahidjo government and launched numerous terrorist attacks within Cameroon (Levine, 1971).

Terrorism, in Cameroon, was reduced to isolated banditry because the UPC did not gain popular support. Terrorism became the tactic of the weak. As the leadership of UPC is killed in the 1970s, the government consolidated its power. Quandie, one of the last leaders of the UPC was captured and murdered in 1971. Other UPC members were also executed by the Ahidjo's one-party system. Levine (1971: 129) contended that "this may well mark one of the last gasps of the 15-year-old rebellion" in Cameroon. By 1984, the Ahidjo administration granted amnesty to UPC exiles abroad and more than 100 members came back to Cameroon without bloodshed. However, Legun (1981) reported that Cameroon since then had experienced two coup attempts with an untold substantial number of deaths.

The situation described in Cameroon explains terrorism in a peripheral West African state. There was no evidence of international terrorism. The same situation in Cameroon is a mirror image of what happens in other West African states such as Nigeria and Ghana. Internal terrorism mostly caused by political repression of opposition leaders and groups exist in these nations. When these governments execute or murder citizens, they do not label their actions as terrorist, rather, they claim patriotism or the often-used phrase such as the "unity of the nation" as the reason to repress political opponents. On the other hand, political opponents, as in Cameroon, are labeled rebels or terrorists that murder governmental officials to achieve their selfish political interests and power.

This case study of terrorism in the periphery demonstrates that the labeling of terrorism still depends on who acts and who has power to define. The point to be made is that terrorism is labeled in the core, periphery, and semiperiphery identically. The labeling of terrorism is based upon the interests of who is doing the labeling. In Cameroon, the interest of the government is power; that is, the power to retain and maintain a one-party system and subsequently to suppress and repress opposition for the sake of this goal. In Moscow, the interest is to destabilize western democracies and suppress and repress regimes opposed to communist principles. In the core, the interest is economic expansion (e.g., RSA) and strategic importance (e.g., Israel) and the elimination of communism and the installation of a democratic system (e.g., Nicaragua).

A Note on the Context of Terrorism in the World System

Terrorism still remains a rarity in West African states. Despite that reality, political relationships in colonial West Africa in particular, and Africa in general, were inherently those of inequality. Colonialism, imperialism, and neocolonialism are forms of political, economic, and cultural domination and control. These systems of domination initiated oppression in African states that until today creates situations ripe for terrorism. Terrorism was, therefore, a part of the colonial system. Both the oppressor and the oppressed used it. It was and is still used as an instrument of power. Criminologists must, therefore, look for another paradigm shift in the study of terrorism. It is suggested that emphasis be placed on the history of colonialism as a system of oppression in the study of terrorism.

Finally, criminologists should approach the study of terrorism in the context of power differentials in the WS. It is suggested that capitalism and socialism are all labels just as terrorism is a label placed on a certain behavior. Focusing on only socialism and capitalism alone as the basis of analysis begs the question. I have tried to incorporate both views without bias. In a new global world order, what is good and beneficial in both economic systems must be incorporated in the study of terrorism. Moreover, it is not only the economic system per se that determines the labeling of terrorism, rather, the definition of terrorism depends on who has the power to decide. The case studies reported in this book in different WS locations buttress such a view.

Conclusion

This chapter used case studies to illustrate different situations in which terrorism has been labeled in the WS. It was argued that the definition and labeling of terrorism depends on who acts and who has the power to define. It is suggested that criminologists may look for a new paradigm shift in the study of terrorism.

7. Inter-Continental Terrorism

Introduction

Terrorism, a pejorative term, is no longer only an act of brutal violence that happens overthere, it indeed happens everywhere. It is a global problem. The terror of gunfire, bombs, guerrilla warfare, insurgencies, ethnic violence in contemporary society, is globalized. Schweitzer (1998) provided a detailed description of the globalization of terrorism and the globalization of weapons expertise. With the collapse of the Soviet Empire, and a failing economy, Soviet scientists are on the lists of rogue states. With the desperate financial burden of Russia and its companion lawlessness, Schweitzer fears the proliferation of nuclear skills in the hands of warlords and nihilist terrorists who will do whatever it takes to acquire dangerous weapons. If they do, technology at their disposal, becomes a volatile weapon. This chapter examines superterrorism and other forms of global terrorism in the world today.

Superterrorism

Schweitzer (1998: 290) defines superterrorism as:

> ... The committing of violent acts using advanced technological tools to cause massive damage to populations and/or to public and private support networks.

In his book, *Superterrorism*, he included chemical and biological agents; plastic explosives and cyber attacks against electronic networks play vital roles in the economic, security, and emergency life of society. Excluded in his definition are minor poisoning incidents or nuclear agents packed around explosives (Schweizer, 1998: 20 and 290). Schweitzer contends that the West fears more of the loosening of the Soviet nuclear technology than it cares for the introduction of democracy and Adam Smith's laissez faire capitalism to the world. Begley (1996) concurs with this form of analysis and argued that the demise of the Soviet Empire has dramatically increased the likelihood of nuclear proliferation. In her analysis, stockpiles of nuclear materials are inadequately monitored and protected against backyard trading. According to Begley (1996: 27), this posits a security nightmare since:

> Even a crude atomic bomb [in the hands of rogue states] could level buildings for miles around ground zero. The resulting fireball would radiate at the speed of sound, incinerating every bit of steel, concrete and human flesh in its path and igniting a holocaust that would make Dresden look like birthday candle.

Begley pointed out that the technology of violence couldn't be compared with the terrorist incidents such as the bombing of the World Trade Center in New York in 1993. A technological attack would be more devastating than bombing. Other scholars have also expressed similar concerns. Laqueur (1987) calls attention to what he referred to as the "Sarajevo effect," a situation by which a terrorist attack may lead to another world war. Wardlaw (1988) asserted that the greatest danger facing the world today is the technology of terrorism and that crazy terrorists who enjoy the thrill of killing may not be deterred by how many people would die. In his view, many terrorist organizations are clamoring for world revolution and may utilize any instrument of mass destruction to achieve their terrorist objectives.

Clark's (1980) typology stipulated that technology provides new avenue for terrorism to thrive and makes terrorism an issue in the future. According to his thesis, America is especially vulnerable to technocratic terrorism, and like Begley (1996), Clark contended that America has not paid adequate attention to technological terrorism. Clark (1980) warned that nuclear facilities are not properly controlled; transportation systems for nuclear and chemical material lack desirable security; and production facilities and chemical agents are vulnerable to terrorists. White (1991:268) indicated correctly that some experts on terrorism tend to focus on "attacks on technological installations, the use of chemical and biological weapons, and the use of radioactive material and nuclear weapons." Should technological terrorism materialize, no society would be immune from it. Such an attack would create problems for the WS (White, 1991).

Laquer (1987) underscored the importance of the threat of nuclear terrorism when he strongly claimed that nuclear terrorism could lead to inter-continental crisis. For example, a confrontation between Israel and the PLO may lead to a deeper crisis between US and Russia if Israel is a target of nuclear attack by the PLO (Vetter and Perlstein, 1991) or any other Middle East surrogate state of Russia. There is evidence that the nuclear club is no longer within the control of the USA and Russia and other countries such as China, England, and France. Most semi-peripheral and peripheral societies feel that it is unfair for the West and East to arrogate nuclear technology only to themselves. Libya, India, Pakistan, North Korea, Iraq, are among states that are suspected of possessing nuclear technology or are anxious to acquire the weapon. In fact, Iraq has used chemical weapons on the Kurds as well as on its citizens (Vetter and Perlstein, 1991).

The cold war remnants of military stockpiles by both Russia and America makes the availability of nuclear agents in the hands of other countries much more feasible. Alexander (1983) indicated that the availability of fissionable material avails the terrorists the opportunity to steal nuclear agents from leftover nuclear stockpiles. The Internet now makes it possible for the dissemination of information on how to manufacture nuclear bombs, which will help the terrorists to construct their dream bombs. Unless seriously checked by combined efforts by America and Russia, the world would be a more dangerous place to live in the twenty-first century. More and more semiperipheral and peripheral nations are seeking nuclear capabilities. It seems that the only way a country is respected in the international community depends on her ability to lunch long range nuclear missiles. No wonder then these countries are hungry for nuclear strength. The proliferation of nuclear agents may end up in the wrong hands.

It is obvious that some peripheral society leaders like to stay in office forever and such weapons in their hands would undoubtedly lead to ethnic genocide. In Africa, for instance, leaders like to stay forever in office. Togo, Zaire, Nigeria, Liberia, and many others have witnessed the unwillingness of political, self-proclaimed, and thin-gods to vacate office. Iraq is a current example and Sadam's greed to conquer Kuwait led to the Gulf War. Imagine, what would have happened if Sadam Hussein had the nuclear capability. Definitely, such a military weapon would have been utilized against Kuwait, Saudi Arabia, Israel and American soldiers. Superterrorism, in short, connotes danger for the peace and well being of the international community.

Global Terrorism

The world we live in today is simply a small international community. What affects one society directly or indirectly affects another society. In business, military, education, and economic cooperation such as one Europe and NAFTA, it is evident that the world is becoming one global village. As coined here, global terrorism refers to glocal terrorism (i.e., localization of terrorism) which connotes the use of violence by a dissident group or nation to avenge against the actions of a core state in peripheral or semiperipheral country or conjugal nation allied to the core country in other to achieve a stated mission. Glocal terrorism can equally come in the form of core nuclear states utilization of their technology weapons against peripheral and semiperipheral nations. Iraq's use of scud missiles against Israel, an ally of the US, during the Gulf war demonstrates Iraq's dissatisfaction with America. While Israel was not at war with Iraq, super Scud missiles were launched against the state of Israel from Iraq showing that the world is villagized or glocalized due to the availability of technological weapons. If China punishes Taiwan with its super weapons of mass destruction, that may constitute terroristic act of violence and other military powers may be dragged in the mess.

To further illustrate the glocal nature of inter-continental terrorism, the near-simultaneous attacks on U.S. embassies in Nairobi, Kenya, and Dar es Salaam, Tanzania, provide excellent examples. The ABC News reported on January 8, 1999 that 224 people, including 12 Americans were killed in the two explosions. This means that inter-continental terrorists target areas where expectations of terrorist attacks are minimum. While the terrorists were angry at America, Africans in Kenya and Tanzania were murdered in their own homelands. These dead Africans were not concerned or were ignorant about the mission of the transnational terrorists but had to die where God originally planted them for nothing but terrorist vengeance against the U.S.

In August 1999, writing for the ABCNEWS, MacVicar reported that the U.S. Tomahawk cruise missiles destroyed a Sudanese pharmaceutical factory to pieces in retaliation for the aforementioned embassy bombings. The reason given by the White House was that the plant was used to manufacture chemical weapons at the direction of Osama bin Laden who was charged with masterminding the bombings in Nairobi and Dar es Salaam. Again, what bin laden did has direct consequences on the Sudanese workers who depended on the plant for employment and medicine for their respective families. MacVicar (1999) indicated that before the Idris' Al-Shifa plant was flattened, it produced 50 percent of the Sudanese medicine. According to MacVicar (1999:2) " a highly classified Pentagon review concludes that the decision to bomb was based on bad intelligence."

Osama bin Laden has been described as a devout Muslim, brave, educated, and rich (Newsweek 1999; Ransport 1999). He is an ascribed member of the richest family in Saudi Arabia and resides presently in Afghanistan. He has been declared as one of the most wanted international terrorists in the world by the U.S. (Newsweek 1999; Ransport 1999). Bin Laden prides himself as a peacemaker while to the U.S. and allies, he represents a "borderless terrorist." Bin Laden and his Fatwa Islamic fundamentalist movement were implicated in the attacks against the U.S. military barracks in Riyadh in November 1995 and Dharan in June 1996 and both incidents claimed 24 American lives with over one hundred injured people. The antecedents of these attacks were attributed to the U.S. involvement in the Gulf War with Iraq and the suffering of the Iraq people because of the sanctions imposed against Iraq by the United Nations (Ransport 1999).

Bin Laden declared war against the United States in 1996 for championing the Christian-Zionist conspiracy against Muslims as he claimed. The Fatwa movement is purely against the Israeli occupation of Jerusalem which must be recaptured by the Islamic forces. As a self-proclaimed peacemaker, bin Laden's mission is to restore Islam to its traditional glory which will lead to a lasting peace. He views the U.S. presence in Saudi Arabia as a military occupation of the sacred land. To bin Laden and his followers, Saudi Arabia is under siege and the U.S. is there to zap the economic resources of the Arabian Peninsula. He justifies his ideology in terms of self-defense against oppressors unsympathetic to the Muslim cause (Ransport 1999; Newsweek 1999). Bin Laden and his multi-ethnic fundamentalist revolutionaries are well trained in guerrilla warfare; adequately better funded than most other Islamic revolutionaries; and operate in cells which make capture and detection difficult for the

U.S. agencies such as the FBI. Ransport (1999:1) puts it in the following manner:

> ... Moreover, these "Arab Afghans," natives of Algeria, Egypt, Jordan, Libya, Morocco, Saudi Arabia, Tunisia, and Yemen among others, operate in flexible and loosely defined ad hoc cellular structures when deployed on terrorist missions. This permeable "structure" makes it that much more difficult for intelligence and security authorities to monitor their movements and to unravel their connection with one another.

As the evidence above demonstrates, bin Laden was not born in East Africa and his cause is not an African cause. However, the missions of Fataw have directly affected adversely innocent citizens of Africa in Sudan, Kenya, and Tanzania. The bombing of these African cities by bin Laden and the U.S. Embassies demonstrate the glocal nature of terrorism in the WS. The world is like a glocal village. An action against one village affects the other village in an inter-connected world. This is what I label glocal or global terrorism. On the other hand, the intention is not to minimize the documented evidence that Sudan provided safe heavens for terrorist academies of the Islamic fundamentalists. As Kushner (1998) points out, Sudan maintained terrorist training grounds for the Palestinian Islamic Jihad (PIJ), the Lebanese Hezbollah (Party of God), the Islamic Resistant Movement (Hamas), and other Iranian supported-terrorist organizations. Due to these terrorist camps in Sudan, Sudan was added in the U.S. Department's short list as one of the states that sponsored terrorism in 1993.

At the time of writing this chapter, it was again reported that Osama bin Laden is planning another terrorist attack against U.S. Embassies in Africa and that the U.S. intelligence has no knowledge of the timing and the target of the operation. Rather, bin Laden has been placed on the FBI's 10 Most Wanted List of fugitives (The Daily Times 1999: 4). The essential curiosity is why bin Laden and his associates have selected African nations for terrorist operations? It maybe that bin Laden and company realize that the U.S. government, the state department in particular, has left the American Embassies in Africa vulnerable for terrorist attacks. Africa has therefore become a hotbed for ideological warfare. By striking U.S. targets successfully in Africa, the terrorist is still achieving its objectives even if only few Americans die in the process.

Bin Laden has no regard for human life while many Africans suffer with indirect humiliation of the United States.

If bin Laden and his organization get their hands on biological and other technological weapons, the destruction of life and property that will result from it shall undoubtedly surpass what happened in Kenya and Tanzania. This type of vengeance against the U.S., in my view, is totally unwarranted. Osama bin Laden's erratic and insane attacks with technology of weapons could threaten global security. Russia's underhanded maneuver by first placing its military in Kosovo peace making demonstrates that we are still in an unsafe world. With her legion of military capabilities, Russia will always demand respect in the international community by flexing its military muscles. This means that there is always a threat that Russia will support rogue states when U.S. tries to remedy wrongs as exhibited in Kosovo. The threat of a nuclear war is still feasible and the fragile friendship between the U.S. and Russia is not sufficient to curb a technological war disaster.

What shall be done is to locate Osama bin Laden and prevent his attacks before negotiations are entered into between the members of the nuclear club. This can be achieved by violating even a country's sovereignty since the world will be a safer place in the long run. Crazy terrorists can originate a glocal war. Moreover, African societies must not rely on the U.S. to provide adequate security for its populace. They must elevate their security needs in other to catch terrorists operating in the continent. It is a shame that these African leaders cannot even provide a bare minimum of security for their citizens. They are busy trying to be in power in perpetuity and have forgotten the proper role of governance and the social contract between the rulers and the governed.

Persistent Fear of Global Terrorism

Recently, India and Pakistan have tested successfully their nuclear technology contributing to the growth of more nuclear states. Israel is also counted as a country with undeclared nuclear capability while South Africa tested its nuclear weapons in the Indian Ocean. Some states such as Iran, Iraq and some North African countries have active nuclear testing programs (Jenkins 1998). Proliferation of these weapons of mass destruction has been attributed mainly to the fragmentation of the former

Soviet Union that left a number of states such as Belarus, Ukraine, and Kazakhstan with nuclear weapons. The localization of these weapons in the hands of weak economic states has led to a persistent fear of the threat of terrorism in the world. Not all scholars are in agreement with this claim.

Arkin (1997:37) documented arguments against the view that the decline of the Soviet Empire led to nuclear proliferation.

> The number of weapons that are operational today is less than half of the number just ten years ago. Only a handful of warheads are been produced worldwide (contrasted with a 5,000 annual production rate a decade ago).... Fewer than a dozen nuclear storage sites remain outside the homelands of the nuclear powers.

Jenkins (1998) wrote that the world experienced more terrorism in the 1970s than today but also pointed out that terrorism is bloodier in the WS today than in the past. It all means that citizens of the global society are more likely to die as in Tanzania and Kenya than ever before. Terrorists are more dangerous with nuclear weapons than ordinary shootings and and mushroom bombing. The world is not a more peaceful society if the FBI is constantly worried about bin Laden and his followers and the type of dangerous arsenals they might have acquired. The hard reality is that nuclear agents are more available to rogue states and terrorists than at any era in history.

Others have pointed out that the US and Russia, since the end of the Cold War, have insisted on ambitious programs of nuclear disarmament. Mendelson (1992) asserted that arms control agreements between the nuclear powers proves to be effective in deterring nuclear proliferation in the Middle East and South Asia. Nonproliferation Treaty of the 1970s was cited as a good example of measures that will be adopted to curb the spread of nuclear technology. Sokolski (1992) proposed that nuclear export controls have been and continues to be effective in the prevention of nuclear proliferation. Sokolski advocated tougher punishment such as imprisonment for corporate officials who engage in the supply and transfer of nuclear materials which could assist in the development of nuclear technology.

However, Leventhal (1992) countered the argument that export control mechanisms are weak and could not prevent or delay the transfer of nuclear materials which would lead to the production of dangerous weapons. Leventhal contended that these weak controls have permitted some countries to acquire uranium, plutonium, and other materials necessary for the production of nuclear weapons. Basically, rogue nations are clamoring to have nuclear capabilities which makes the world more dangerous. The fear of global terrorism is real since terrorists may be willing to use these weapons for ideological gains. It is this type of proliferation of nuclear technology that makes glocal terrorism real in the minds of terrorism observers.

Conclusion

The threat of nuclear terrorism is real. The U.S. is presently debating the importance of constructing a sky defense system that will prevent rogue states from striking U.S. territories with nuclear missiles. Efforts must be made by the global society to stop the massive production and proliferation of nuclear weapons for the security of humankind.

8. Summary, Racial and Global Terrorism

Introduction

The objective of this chapter is to use the Republic of South Africa (RSA) as a qualitative and contextual example, which illustrates the theoretical positions taken throughout this book. Readers will after comprehending the contents of this chapter, grasp the difficulties scholars encounter with the definition of terrorism and also to realize why it is necessary to re-define terrorism in the WS. First the discussion will focus on racial terrorism and global apartheid. Finally, an attempt will be made to provide an argument for the criminalization of terrorism.

Racial Terrorism and Global Apartheid

The theoretical argument addressed in this book is that there are two faces of terrorism in the WS. Unfortunately, however, conventional scholars have only alluded to that type of terrorism that works against the state's interest. This means that powerful core nations who shape what constitutes acts of terrorism disregard official terrorism practiced by sovereign states even though it is the most precarious form of terrorism. This argument will be clearly addressed and expanded upon in this concluding chapter by examining racial terrorism as practiced in South Africa.

Racial Terrorism

The so-called pseudo Republic of South Africa (RSA) claimed legitimacy in its regime by assuming the role of a republic. This means that elected representatives govern the country. Those who support the racial ideology of this republic believe that RSA practices a constitutional democracy. At the same time, the government officials were elected by only the votes of the minority settler (white) population. The majority of blacks was denied full electoral standing and as a result did not participate in the democracy. By definition therefore, RSA was a racist republic. However, the term "republic" gives legitimacy to this apartheid regime in South Africa whenever the phrase is used. This chapter posits that a government that uses terrorism to achieve its political goals does not practice a constitutional democracy. Democracy by definition is popular participation by the majority, usually through voting, in governmental decision-making and the choice of governmental leaders (Hatcher, 1961; Levy, 1982).

What is important in a democracy is the recognition of the people and their ability to participate in a nation's decision making without being restricted by its laws. Leaders of a democratic society must accept failures to perform a task or fulfill an obligation when necessary. Not allowing blacks to vote was a default in RSA's government that must be acknowledged by its leaders. Moreover, they must accept all the population as equals before the law. Finally, democratic societies must maintain a common ground whereby different viewpoints, interests, and values can be compromised (Levy, 1982; Hatcher, 1961).

Using artificial ideals of democracy to validate terrorism is not tolerable. The RSA practiced an empty democracy. The government was bound to fail since the majority of the people were denied freedom, economic, and political rights. The majority of the people were denied justice and political membership. Thus, the government lacked a safety valve that was needed to sustain a democracy. Rather, the government used different kinds of criminal acts of terrorism to achieve its apartheid goals.

The RSA utilized criminal acts of terrorism against Africans. The massacre of Blacks at Sharpeville was terroristic. The indiscriminate shooting of unarmed civilians are, in the words of Panunzio, "criminal acts of terrorism" (Gregor, 1982). This view is expanded upon below. State-sponsored terrorism in South Africa took different forms. The South African regime employed torture, detention without trial, political imprisonment, etc., to achieve its terrorism objectives. It sponsored violence against blacks and used legal terrorism against Africans.

Oruka (1985: 105) maintained "legal terrorism is always a state inspired practice...." An action or practice is classified as legal if it is recognized and granted the authority of the state. For example, Joseph Mdluli was tortured and murdered by the Durban Security Police in March

1976. Steve Biko, the Black Consciousness Leader, was murdered in September 1977. Samuel Mugivhela Tshikhudo died in the hands of the security police in 1984 (see Amnesty International Report, 1984, 1985, 1986, 1987; Davenport, 1987).

The RSA had different laws (Communism Act, Terrorism Act, and Anti-sabotage Acts etc.) to suppress, repress, oppress, terrorize, torture, and murder opponents of apartheid. They were passed to depict Blacks as communists and terrorists in order to maintain continuous support from the core nations.

In a way, the racist government of South Africa succeeded. For example, the U.S. State Department has proclaimed Iran, Libya, Cuba, North Korea, South Yemen, and the former Soviet Union as states that sponsored terrorism (Poland, 1988). RSA was not among the list identified. The question is why is this distinction made? The constructive engagement policy of the Reagan Administration in the 1980s supports such assertion. From an African worldview, such policy accepts the legitimization of imperialism, colonialism, and neocolonialism. When a core nation involves itself in the WS on the pretext of economic interests, the legitimate rights of the peripheral peoples become secondary. The popular perspective is that what is good for the core is good for the peripheral. Therefore, by supporting the terrorist government of South Africa, it is also in the best interest of blacks that are deprived of political and economic power in the land of their fathers.

In short, RSA was referred to as a "contested area" of the world between the former USSR and the U.S.A. Crocker (1981) viewed the African National Congress (ANC) as a threat to the Western Alliance and referred to ANC as a terrorist organization.

At this point, any reader will understand the purpose of this argument. Terrorism, or what constitutes it, is in the eyes of the beholder. For some, the RSA is not a terrorist state since it legitimates its war against the ANC as a war against terrorism. Those who subscribe to and support such a perspective may be doing so in there own national interests since the scarce resources of the RSA is at issue. On the other hand, those who support the ANC as freedom fighters who are fighting liberation wars may be doing so in order to justify the existence and inalienable rights of the majority black population. Whichever way one looks at it, the two faces of terrorism emerge in the WS as an ultimate example of the global economic struggle for scarce resources.

On one hand, it must not be ignored that the settler minority regime in South Africa refers to the liberation forces (the ANC) as terrorists. This is because the liberation forces (as an organization not a state) possess no authority or legitimacy to impose punishment on the members of the settler regime. On the other hand, the minority regime, operating as a sovereign state, has the authority and legitimacy to inflict punishment on liberation forces. Again, it is this one particular issue that led to the rejection of the traditional definition of terrorism in this study. Because of this question of authority and legitimacy, it becomes difficult to argue that South Africa used law to terrorize the black majority.

This view is rejected here, however. Rather, the view taken is just as Adolf Hitler used law to terrorize Jews, the minority regime (which in fact supported Nazism) in South Africa used law to coerce the majority population into submission. It is crucial to say that such a law was not without threat and violence to blacks, which were the object of coercion. By passing those laws directed only against blacks, the South African regime made it clear that a terrorist can have law (regardless of state authority and legitimacy). Based on this argument the behavior of the RSA must be labeled as terrorism. As Fanon might argue, if the RSA chooses violence then it is natural for the ANC also to use violence to achieve its own political and economic objectives. The WS participates in and facilitates this form of racial, legitimate terrorism. The RSA's rigid principle of economic domination in South Africa has been supported by the core and has been transformed into a sort of global apartheid.

Global Apartheid

The point of global apartheid rests on the premise that core countries such as Britain, U.S.A., Germany and Japan have played a significant economic role in sustaining and maintaining the institutionalization of apartheid in South Africa. The RSA's relationships to Britain, the U.S.A., Germany, and Japan, are extremely difficult to understand. In the area of global division of labor, the RSA is strategically important as a mineral supplier for industrial production in the core nations (Davenport, 1987; Danaher, 1984).

For example, there are between 2,000 and 2,500 foreign owned companies in South Africa. The largest number, a total of 1,200 are British, 350 belong to Germany, followed by the 340 U.S. owned and controlled companies. Total foreign investment in apartheid enterprises in the region is apparently $30 billion U.S. dollars (Danaher, 1984;

Davenport, 1987). In short, about 20 percent of all manufacturing industry in South Africa is foreign owned. Therefore, it can be concluded that the global market controlled by the core societies support apartheid capitalism. The historical antecedents of this process also demonstrate the core's role in RSA's apartheid regime.

Perdue (1988) reported that in the late nineteenth century, U.S. engineers built the RSA's mining industry. American companies provided mining equipment and managed the mines (Danaher, 1984). By the latter part of the nineteenth century, U.S. firms such as Singer Sewing Machine, Kidder, Peabody Co., Mobil, and General Electric established business corporations in South Africa (Perdue, 1988). Ford and Kodak followed them. U.S. companies developed metals, the motor industry, agricultural equipment, and petrochemicals (Danaher, 1984). Despite interruptions, U.S. companies have exported computers and other advanced technology that the South African police and military used in the maintenance of the rigid principles of apartheid (Perdue, 1988). In fact, Danaher (1984) reported that corporations such as General Electric, Honeywell, and Allis-Chalmers helped to develop South Africa's nuclear weapons. According to the World Almanac (1985) West Germany, Japan and the U.S., were South Africa's leading trading partners while Britain, under Thatcher, opposed economic sanctions against the RSA.

Recently, however, the U.S. government (in the past decade) encouraged businesses to divest in South Africa. Between 1986 and 1987, 96 U.S. companies detached their direct investment ties to South Africa leaving a total of 167 firms intact (Perdue, 1988). But the economy of South Africa still has unrestricted access to U.S. products and technology. This is because most firms including GM and IBM left the country in name only. They maintained licensing and other agreements with their business subsidiaries. Core involvement in South Africa is complex and difficult to understand because these corporations have been joint partners of the RSA monopolies and government in the exploitation of the natural and human resources of the African people.

The "constructive engagement doctrine" of the Reagan Administration, referred to earlier was based on the idea that all Africans will benefit through a private sector system in South Africa. Crocker (1981) argued that "with the right mix of aid, policy reform, and a strongly reinvigorated role for the private sector, African peoples will opt for the growth and freedom . . . inherent in the free worlds international economic system." In short, Crocker's position can be interpreted to mean that through neocolonialism (characterized by multinational corporations), economic growth will emerge and apartheid will gradually be eliminated so as to benefit Africans. Again, from an African perspective, Crocker's argument lacks substance. He seems to be saying that what benefits the plantation system benefits the slaves. This argument makes no sense to the oppressed (e.g., see Fanon, 1968). It made no sense to those who suffered under Jim Crowism in the U.S., and it makes no sense to those suffering the effects of grand apartheid in South Africa.

Jim Crowism and Grand Apartheid

The purpose of this section is to demonstrate the differences between Jim Crowism and grand apartheid. Both are systems of racial segregation and domination in the WS power arrangement. Both systems were used to oppress and suppress blacks in their different WS locations.

Three notable studies conducted in the U.S. argued that the system of apartheid couldn't be compared with the system of segregation that occurred in the southern regions of the United States (Greenberg, 1980; Fredickson, 1981; Cell, 1982). In other words, it would be wrong to equate the apartheid program to the Jim Crow laws that existed in various regions of the U.S.A. for nearly a century. Jim Crow laws were most pronounced in the Southern region of the. U.S. Both systems of segregation are not equal but similar in intent. Jim Crow was a system of legal segregation and suppression of blacks used to legally exclude blacks from voting booths. Unlike South Africa, which has no conditions of any kind that will qualify a black adult to vote, such conditions existed in the U.S. For example, in 1890, Mississippi established three permanent devices for voting. These included a residence requirement, the payment of a poll tax, and the ability to read or interpret a state constitution. South Carolina added to these requirements a list of crimes such as larceny, which disenfranchised the offender. Many Southern states found the good-character test particularly useful for excluding blacks from the polls; an applicant seeking to vote must produce a responsible person to verify his or her character (Newby, 1978; Quarles, 1964).

Also, white primary laws were passed, claiming that the Democratic Party was a voluntary association, which had the right to limit voting, as it desired in party elections. The South used the grandfather clause to keep blacks voteless (Newby, 1978). In comparison, the grand apartheid system, as practiced in the RSA, is "the broad geographical separation of peoples on a basis of equal rights within their respective territories" (Davenport, 1987: 542). The key difference between Jim Crow Laws in the U.S.A. and Grand Apartheid Acts in South Africa is that under South African law, blacks had never been granted citizenship.

The minority regime of South Africa for the past several years has reluctantly given up some of the edifice of apartheid policies. It has, however, maintained the central focus of apartheid, "a denial of meaningful political power to the country's black majority" (Political Handbook of the World, 1989: 551). Blacks are also excluded from economic participation. For example blacks cannot own landed property in areas reserved for whites.

Another difference between Jim Crowism and grand apartheid in RSA is related to the use of force. Under Jim Crowism, the National Guard was used to maintain peaceful civil right demonstrations or to use force when necessary. Under Grand Apartheid, South Africa's security forces "were authorized to take any action deemed necessary to counter perceived threats to public safety, with full exemption from subsequent legal prosecution" (Political Handbook of the World, 1989: 549). This has led to uncontrolled state violence directed against blacks in the RSA. The re-imposition of the State of Emergency was in line with the government's desire to stop black people by any means from commemorating the 1976 Soweto rioting (Davenport, 1987).

Blacks in America rejected Jim Crowism and protested against hanging and torture against blacks in the U.S. The situation is worse in apartheid South Africa. Blacks in South Africa have had enough of global apartheid. They are no longer willing to bow to its oppression, discrimination and exploitation. They are no longer prepared to be tortured, terrorized and massacred. They are no longer willing to tolerate being treated as strangers in their own father's land. Recent events in South Africa demonstrated that the majority is prepared to match violence with violence. They are willing to die for a worthy struggle, a struggle characterized by the desire to be citizens in their own country. Since the RSA uses violence/terrorism to control and dominate the majority, suppress democratic principles that is the backbone of the core nations, it behooves on the majority to fight, which is the only response to the repressive state machine. Both methods can be viewed as terrorist devices depending on who is doing the defining in the WS. The RSA utilizes institutional terror against blacks as the next section elucidates.

Institutional Terror in RSA

The focus of this section is to show how the RSA used governmental/state terror to extract African labor and control the economic resources of South Africa. Apartheid in RSA is more than a doctrine of racial domination and cultural imperialism. Its main goal has been the authority to manage and dominate the labor market. The dependence of the settler caste on African labor has been documented in South African economic history as reflected in the population disparity between the different races (See Marger, 1985: 203 for details). South Africa was created by imperialism to use Africans as cheap labor power for the sole purpose of exploiting the diamond and gold mines that had been discovered in 1866 and 1884, respectively (Davenport, 1987). The RSA used institutional terror to maintain the inflexible doctrine of apartheid. Thus, as Slovo (1976:139) puts it:

> South Africa was conquered by force and is today ruled by force. At moments when white autocracy feels itself threatened, it does not hesitate to use the gun. When the gun is not in use, legal and administrative terror, fear, social and economic pressures, complacency and confusion generated by propaganda and education are the devices brought into play in an attempt to harness the people's opposition. Behind these devices hovers force whether in reserve or in actual employment force is ever present and this has been so ever since the white man came to Africa.

Originally, the ANC utilized peaceful and non-violent approaches to negotiate with the regime of terror to recognize blacks as humans. But due to the violent nature of the RSA, the ANC adopted the policy of armed struggle after the state massacred 65 innocent protestors, as the only language the regime will be forced to obey. This type of behavior intensifies terrorism in the WS. Whether terrorism is used by liberation fighters or by state officials, it still constitutes criminal activity that must be eliminated.

Criminalization of Terrorism

In this section, the dual faces of terrorism will be examined in an effort to address the issue of criminalizing the behaviors of terrorists, whether or not terrorist acts are perpetrated by powerful actors in the global society or by the oppressed. Terrorism, whether sponsored by states such as RSA or by liberation fighters such as the ANC, constitutes criminal acts of violence. No matter the ideological reasons, murder is murder regardless of the cause. Therefore, terrorism is murder and must be criminalized. Terrorism in my view is criminal activity. Any criminal act of terrorism such as the bombing of the World Trade Center in New York that resulted in the killing of innocent people or the use of state secret police to destroy the lives of people in South Africa must be equated to murder and other crimes of violence such as theft and kidnapping. In short, any government or groups willing to kill in order to support its political and religious ideologies can be labeled a terrorist. Thus, this must consist of governments as well as guerrillas. Terrorist acts of violence can be perpetrated by governments from above to oppress the citizens by using policies of terror, or from below by revolutionary or freedom fighters who adopt different methods of terror to oppose the political establishment.

State Sponsored Terror or Terrorism From Above

Earlier in this book, a distinction was made between official and common terrorism. State sponsored murder is official terrorism. It is the most hazardous form of terrorism. When 65 blacks were murdered by the RSA's secret police in Sharpeville, it constituted a terrorist act of violence. Such behaviors by states must be criminalized. States have no license to destroy human lives or the livelihood of those opposed to the corrupting effects of governmental policies.

A good example of terrorism from above exists in Latin American countries. Citizens have regularly vanished without trace during the past decade in Argentina, Uruguay, Chile, and Brazil. Death squads have also existed in Guatemala, Brazil, and Argentina to help officials carry out their terrorist goals (Stohl, 1988). Stohl asserted that state terrorism in the domestic realm alone is responsible for millions of deaths.

The promotion of such violence must be recognized from the level of a serious criminal act that requires global condemnation. Totalitarian regimes around the world (e.g., Zaire, RSA, Libya, Syria, Iraq, Iran, etc.) allow themselves and their police protegees the monopoly of arms and the use of force. When a dictatorship owns terrorism, all other forms of violence except those sanctioned by the state are outlawed and opponents are quickly silenced. This implies that governments that use terrorism against citizens are less likely to be terrorized than pure democratic states. The former Soviet Union had a monopoly over its force, and was less vulnerable to internal violence.

The point is that states have the money, the technology, the information systems, the intelligence operations and support that makes state terrorism more treacherous than terrorists from below. Murder by states must therefore be criminalized regardless of the legitimacy accorded to states as sovereign nations.

Common Terrorism/Guerrilla Warfare or Terrorism from Below

Although Franz Fanon, in his many books already cited throughout this book, presented violence as liberation, terrorism from below in the form of guerrilla warfare or freedom fighters also constitutes criminality. Fanon's work on violence influenced Third World revolutionaries.   In Fanon's words, "at the level of individuals, violence is a cleansing force. It frees (the oppressed) from his inferiority complex and from his despair and inaction." Therefore, liberation fighters understood Fanon's philosophy of violence that was embraced by the colonized as a necessary means to fight the oppressor.

Terrorists such as Abu Nidal and Mohammad Abbas are threats to innocent people whether they are flying the airplanes or shopping at commercial facilities. The killing and kidnapping of government officials, servicemen and women are terroristic and such behavior by terrorists must also be criminalized. Again murder is murder and must be subjected to the criminal law principles of all nations. So far, it has been argued that terrorism is a criminal activity regardless of whether it is violence from above or from below. What follows is a long quote on suggestions for future research adapted from Crenshaw (1992) and a brief conclusion of Chapter Eight.

Suggestions for Future Research

It has been pointed out previously that scholars have for long studied issues identical to terrorism because terrorism historically has been likened to a form of warfare. Issues such as guerrilla warfare, and civil violence are similar to terrorism. Academics interested in terrorism must try to focus on terrorism alone and develop empirical methodology that will be used to study terrorism. In order to develop an adequate theory of terrorism, a sound research mechanism is needed. Terrorism is a complex issue. Studies must also stress the importance of unobtrusive measures based on case studies that will provide the logical acuity to deal with the important and delicate subjective issue of terrorism.

Crenshaw (1992: 8-9) provided several suggestions that aid in focusing terrorism research in these directions:

1. Research should focus on shifts from nonviolent political action to terrorism and vice versa. That is, the transition points or thresholds in society and in international politics. When does terrorism begin and when does it end? Is there a "life cycle" of terrorism?

2. Changes in the processes or stages of violence overtime, such as shifts from violent protest to terrorism or from terrorism to internal war or regional conflict, should also be investigated. Why do actors switch from one mode of violence to another? Why is terrorism preferred compared with what alternatives? What are the incentives for choosing different violent strategies? Is it solely a question of resources?

3. There is a need for study of the mix of instrumental and expressive or emotional motives in specific groups that use terrorism. Such case studies should provide detailed analysis of leadership, organizational structures, resources, recruitment, mobilization, ideology, and justifications in-groups that use violence. In dismissing the idea that terrorism is pathological, analysts should not ignore the role of psychological factors, but they should be considered as they relate to strategic rationales for terrorism.

4. Similarly, studies of conflict resolution should situate conflict resolution processes (the bargaining inherent in negotiations) within the political context. In particular, researchers should ask if terrorism could be reduced even when the underlying conflict of interests are not resolved. When does terrorism end as a result of bargaining between governments and non-states? When do attempts to resolve conflict lead to increased terrorism?

5.   There should be a greater appreciation of the heterogeneity of political violence. Researchers should concentrate on developing explanations of categories of political violence rather than general theories. Analyses that combine disparate phenomena can only produce confused results. We need focused comparisons of cases that are fundamentally similar. For terrorism researchers, a central problem is the development of a satisfactory typology of terrorism. It may not be possible to speak of terrorism as a homogeneous category.

6.   Researchers should analyze public perceptions of and reactions to terrorism, including the attitudes of both participants and external audiences and with reference to state and insurgent terrorism. How does terrorism affect conceptions of internal and external security? How does the threat of terrorism compare to other social risks?

7.   There is a need for more study of the consequences and outcomes of violence, especially analysis of whether violence succeeds in attaining the goals actors set for it. When does violence--whether terrorism, rebellion, protest, or war--succeed? How frequent are unintended consequences? What difference do they make to outcomes? When is violence an important source of political change?

8.   The interactions between governments and violent oppositions and of adversarial extremist movements against each other (not just the strategies of one or the other in isolation) should be analyzed.

Conclusion

This chapter basically used the RSA as a case study to examine the two faces of terrorism in the WS. It was demonstrated that core nations support the unbending principles of apartheid capitalism in South Africa by engaging in global apartheid because of the scarce resources provided by the RSA's economy. The position taken was that the RSA was not a democracy since it denied the majority of the population their inalienable rights to vote and used violence and torture to suppress the spirit of the opposition. Finally, an attempt was made to criminalize the behavior of terrorists whether violence is from above or below in the WS's distribution of power. The argument addressed is that terrorism is a criminal activity such as murder in the streets is a crime and must be subjected to the same legal criminal codes of nations.

The bombing of the World Trade Center in New York demonstrates the need to study terrorism and its relation to the WS. It shows that the specter of political terrorism is still haunting the world. Terrorism experts speculated about which different terrorist groups (e.g., Balkan factions, Palestinian factions, Iran, Iraq, Libya, and Russian Nationalists) may have caused the explosion at the World Trade Center in New York before the perpetrators were identified. International terrorism in the 1980s was primarily fueled by the cold war but declined due to the rise of Gorbachev to power in the former USSR (Golan, 1990).

However, the end of the cold war has contributed to new international rivalries that have generated acts of terrorism. For example, Russian nationalists who are displeased with what is happening in the former Yugoslavia would like to install a reactionary regime in Moscow. These nationalists also blame Russia's recent problems (corruption, crime, and economic decline) on Western and mainly U.S. influence. Recently, Russian nationalists tried to impeach President Boris Yeltsin from office demanding that he distance himself from free enterprise system and western-oriented diplomacy. In frustration, the Russian reactionaries, nationalists, or enemies of democracy, may use terrorism to seek publicity on American influential business center in New York.

The same argument is true with the Balkan factions such as the Serbian Liberation Front, Balkan Nationalists, Croatian Militants, Bosnian Muslims, and Serbian Nationalists. The Serbia nationalists, since the end of the cold war, have threatened to bomb Western Europe's nuclear facilities if NATO governments intervene militarily in the former Yugoslavia. The changing face of international relations leaves the United States of America as the only recognized superpower, both economically and militarily in the world. Consequently, for terrorists who wish to draw attention to them or who may wish to get even with the U.S. for intervening in other areas of the world, the U.S. has become a more likely target. In short, it is possible that we are entering a phase of world history where the use of terrorism will increase. It is therefore, important for criminologists not to ignore the phenomenon of terrorism and the behavior of terrorists.

Appendix

Table 1: Comparative Terminology

Role of Nations	Theoratical Perspective				
	World System	Undevelopment Dependency	New Dependency		Development
Controlling	Core	Metropole Center	First World		Developed
Quasi Exploited/ Semicontrolling	semiperiphery	Developing	Second World		Developing
Exploited	Periphery	Dependent	Third World Satellite Nations		Under Developed

Table 2: Snyder and Kick's World System Model

Core Nations	Canada, United States, United Kingdom, Netherlands, Belgium, Luxembourg, France, Switzerland, Spain, Portugal, West Germany, Austria, Italy, Yugoslavia, Greece, Sweden, Denmark, South Africa, Japan, Australia.
Semi-periphery Nations	Venezuela, Peru, Argentina, Uruguay, South Korea, Cuba, Ireland, East Germany, Hungary, Cyprus, Bulgaria, Romania, U.S.S.R., Kenya, Finland, Saudi Arabia, Taiwan, India, Pakistan, Burma, Ceylon, Malaysia, Philippines.
Periphery Nations	Chad, Longo, Burundi, Rwanda, Somalia, Ethiopia, Malagasy Republic, Morocco, Algeria, Tunisia, Libya, Sudan, United Arab Republic, Yemen, Mali, Mauritania, Ghana, Upper Volta, Senegal, Dahomey, Niger, Cameroon, Nigeria, Gabon, Central African Republic, Panama, Colombia, Ecuador, Brazil, Bolivia, Paraguay, Chile, North Vietnam, Haiti, Dominican Republic, Mexico, Guatemala, Jamaica, Trinidad and Tobago, Poland, Czechoslovakia, Malta, China (Peoples Republic), Mongolian Republic, Nepal, Thailand, Cambodia, Laos, New Zealand, Iceland, Albania, Syria, Kuwait, Afghanistan, North Korea, South Vietnam, Indonesia.

Table 3: Cross-Classification of Societies by Techno-Economic Heritage and World System Status

Techno-Economic Heritage	World System Status			
	Semiperiphery		Periphery	
	Strong	Weak		
Agrarian	Mexico Brazil Argentina South Korea India Philipines Venezuela	Colombia Chile Egypt Pakistan Thailand Malaysia	Guatemala Honduras Nicaragua Costa Rica Panama Ecuador Peru Bolivia Paraguay	Uruguay Morocco Tunisia Lebanon Afghanistan Burma Sri Lanka Cambodia Laos Indonesia
Horticulture	Nigeria	Ghana Zaire Kenya Zambia	Mali Senegal Mauritania Niger Upper Volta Liberia Togo Cameroon Cent. Afr. Rep.	Chad Congo Uganda Tanzania Malawi Malagasy Rep. Dahomey

Adapted from Nolan (1991). Sociological Focus 21:31.

Table 4: World System Position Based upon Snyder and Kick's Classifications with Amendments

Core Nations N=16			
Canada	West Germany	Sweden	Australia
United Kingdom	Austria	Switzerland	Norway
Netherlands	Italy	France	Denmark
Belgium	Yugoslavia	Luxembourg	Greece

Semiperiphery Nations N=34			
Mexico	Cyprus	South Africa	Spain
Brazil	Ireland	Zambia	Portugal
Argentina	Turkey	Kenya	Jordan
South Korea	Finland	Nigeria	Israel
Colombia	Iran	Zaire	Russia
Egypt	Singapore	Ghana	Rumania
Thailand	Iraq	Venezuela	Bulgaria
Malaysia	Spain	Rumania	Hungary
India	Cuba	Philippines	

Periphery Nations N=74			
Guatemala	Mali	Albania	North Korea
Honduras	Senegal	Iceland	Cambodia
Nicaragua	Mauritania	Colombia	Nepal
Costa Rica	Niger	Gabon	Mongolian Rep.
Uruguay	Uppervolta	Yemen	Malta
Morocco	Liberia	U. Arab Rep.	Dominican Rep.
Tunisia	Togo	Sudan	Haiti
Lebanon	Cameroon	Ethiopia	North Vietnam
Panama	Central African Republic	Somalia	Rwanda
Ecuador	Chad	Oman	Burundi

Table 4: World System Position Based upon Snyder and Kick's Classifications with Amendments (contd.)

Peru	Congo	Kuwait	Uganda
Bolivia	Uganda	Bahrain	Poland
Paraguay	Tanzania	Syria	Mauritius
Afghanistan	Malawi	New Zealand	Guyana
Burma	Malagassi Rep.	Jamaica	Pakistan
Sri Lanka	Dahomey	Bahamas	Barbados
Cambodia	Saudi Arabia	Qatar	Trinidad/Tobago
Laos	Taiwan	Indonesia	Algeria

Table 5: Breakdown of Incidents by Region: Asia

Country of Occurrence	Number of Occurrences	Periphery Target	Semiperiphery Target	Core Target	Tactic
1. Afghanistan	1	--	--	1	Kidnapping
2. Fiji	1	1	--	--	Hijacking
3. India	3	1	2	--	Bombing/Attack
4. Japan	1	--	--	1	Bombing
5. Pakistan	26	22	3	1	Bombing
6. Philippines	21	1	--	20	Bombing/Kidnapping Assassination/Attack
7. Singapore	1	--	--	1	Bombing
8. South Korea	1	--	--	1	Attack
9. Sri Lanka	2	--	2	--	Bombing
10. Thailand	1	1	--	--	Bombing
Total	58	25	6	27	

Table 6: Breakdown of Incidents by Region: Europe

Country of Occurrence	Number of Occurrences	Core Target	Semiperiphery Target	Periphery Target	Tactic
1. Austria	4	1	2	1	Bomb/Assa/Attack
2. Belgium	1	--	--	1	Assassination
3. Cyprus	1	1	--	--	Bomb/Assa/Attack
4. France	15	8	1	6	Bomb/Assa/Attack
5. FRG	12	6	6	--	Assa/Attack/Bomb
6. Greece	11	5	4	2	Bomb/Assa/Kidnap /Attack
7. Hungary	1	--	--	1	Assassination
8. Italy	4	3	--	1	Attack/Bomb/Assa
9. Luxembourg	1	1	--	--	Attack
10. Malta	4	4	--	--	Attack/Assa
11. Norway	2	1	1	--	Hostage/Attack
12. Spain	28	27	1	--	Bomb/Attack/Assa
13. Switzerland	2	1	1	--	Attack/Assa
14. UK	11	7	2	2	Bomb/Assa
Total	97	64	16	12	

Table 7: Breakdown of Incidents by Region: Latin America

Country of Occurrence	Number of Occurrences	Core Target	Semiperiphery Target	Periphery Target	Tactic
1. Argentina	1	1	--	--	Bombing
2. Bolivia	6	5	--	1	Attack/Bombing
3. Brazil	1	1	--	--	Kidnapping
4. Chile	14	14	--	--	Kidnap/Hostage/Attack/Bomb
5. Colombia	13	11	--	1	Kidnap/Attack/Bomb/Assa
6. Costa Rica	1	1	--	--	Bombing
7. Cuba	1	--	1	--	Hijacking
8. Dominican Rep.	3	3	--	--	Bombing
9. Haiti	1	1	--	--	Kidnapping
10. Honduras	5	2	1	2	Bomb/Attack/Assa
11. Jamaica	2	2	--	--	Attack
12. Mexico	2	2	--	--	Bomb/Attack
13. Nicaragua	1	1	--	--	Kidnapping
14. Panama	1	--	--	1	Attack
15. Peru	38	31	2	5	Bomb/Attack/Hostage/Assa
16. Suriname	3	3	--	--	Kidnap/Attack
17. Venezuela	5	--	1	4	Attack/Kidnap
Total	97	78	5	14	

Table 8: Breakdown of Incidents by Region: Middle East

Country of Occurrence	Number of Occurrences	Core Target	Semiperiphery Target	Periphery Target	Tactic
1. Chad	1	1	--	--	Bombing
2. Cyprus	3	2	1	--	Bomb/Assa
3. Egypt	2	2	--	--	Attack/Assa
4. Iran	4	1	2	--	Attack/Bomb
5. Iraq	5	3	2	--	Kidnap/Attack
6. Israel	35	3	31	1	Assa/Bomb/Attack
7. Jordan	1	--	--	1	Assassination
8. Kuwait	5	3	--	2	Bomb/Attack
9. Lebanon	41	19	4	18	Kidnap/Bomb/Assa /Attack
10. Mauritania	1	--	--	1	Attack
11. Morocco	1	1	--	--	Kidnapping
12. Saudi Arabia	1	--	--	1	Bombing
13. Sudan	1	1	--	--	Kidnapping
14. Tunisia	4	4	--	--	Bombing
15. Turkey	7	4	2	1	Assa/Bomb/Attack
16. West Bank	1	1	--	--	Attack
Total	113	45	40	28	

Table 9: Breakdown of Incidents by Region: North America

Country of Occurrence	Number of Occurrences	Core Target	Semiperiphery Target	Periphery Target	Tactic Hijack/Bomb/Threat/ Kidnap/Assa
1. United States	8	2	3	3	
Total	8	2	3	3	

Table 10: Breakdown of Incidents by Region: Sub-Saharan Africa

Country of Occurrence	Number of Occurrences	Core Target	Semiperiphery Target	Periphery Target	Tactic
1. Angola	1	1	--	--	Kidnapping
2. Congo	1	--	--	1	Hijacking
3. Djibouti	1	--	--	1	Bombing
4. Ethiopia	3	3	--	--	kidnap/Attack
5. Mozambique	3	3	--	--	Kidnap/Assa
6. Somalia	1	1	--	--	Kidnapping
7. Sudan	1	1	--	--	Kidnapping
8. Swaziland	2	--	2	--	
9. Zambia	1	--	--	1	Bombing
10. Zimbabwe	4	2	--	2	Attack
Total	18	11	2	5	

Table 11: Terrorist Incidents by World System Position of Country of Occurence and World System Position of Target

	# of Countries	# of Incidents	Core Target	Semiperiphery Target	Periphery Target
Core	13	97	64	21	16
Semiperiphery	*9	108	33	.41	24
Periphery	44	192	136	+25	46
Total	66	397	233	87	86

* Based on the Countries designated as block D by Snyder and Kick (1979), RAND Chronology placed Cyprus in Europe and Latin America respectively without explanation. Therefore, in this study, Cyprus counted as two countries. This explains why there is a total of 397 incidents in table eleven rather than 394 as originally recorded by the RAND Chronology. Cyprus when placed in Latin America as did RAND experienced three international terrorist incidents. It also explains why the table indicated nine semiperipheral countries instead of eight.

. 31 targets were directed at Israel alone and Israel has a close relationship with core nations (e.g. U.S., U.K., Canada).

+ Syria was targeted nine times and it is considered a regional power with a controlling influence over Lebanon.

Table 12: Breakdown of International Terrorist Incidents by Region for 1986 and 1987

Middle East	122	113
Latin America	110	98
Europe	123	97
Asia	41	58
Sub-Saharan Africa	7	18
North America	7	18

Table 13: Five Nationalities Most Often Targeted by International Terrorists for 1987

Country	# of Targets	World System Position
United States	121	Core
Israel	35	Semiperiphery
France	25	Core
United Kingdom	22	Core
Pakistan	20	Periphery

Table 14: Ten Nationalities with the Most International Terrorist Incidents for 1987

Country	# of Targets	World System Position
1. Lebanon	41	Semiperiphery
2. Peru	38	Semiperiphery
3. Israel	35	Semiperiphery
4. Spain	28	Core
5. Pakistan	26	Periphery
6. Philippines	21	Periphery
7. France	15	Core
8. Chile	14	Periphery
9. Colombia	13	Periphery
10. FRG	12	Core

Table 15: Cross-Description of Tactic and Region (From the RAND Chronology of International Terrorism, 1987)

	Asia	Europe	Latin America	Middle East	North America	Africa
Kidnapping	5	1	13	24	2	7
Attack	15	28	33	19	--	3
Hijacking	1	--	2	--	1	1
Bombing	34	50	41	50	2	4
Hostage	--	1	5	--	--	--
ASSAS; Shooting	4	19	4	19	1	4
Threat	1	--	--	2	2	--

Table 16: Cross-Description of Target and Region (From the RAND Chronology of International Terrorism, 1987)

	Asia	Europe	Latin America	Middle East	North America	Sub-Saharan Africa
Diplomatic	9	21	29	21	--	--
Business	19	30	34	19	1	3
Military	4	13	2	30	--	--
Police	--	--	--	2	--	--
Airline	2	4	3	2	2	1
Citizen	9	4	7	19	--	1
Energy	1	2	4	3	--	1
Government	--	10	--	--	--	--
Exile	4	7	--	1	--	--
Relig. Ethnic	--	1	17	3	--	1
Maritime	--	--	--	3	--	--
Transportation	6	2	--	4	--	--
Activist, Ter	1	4	1	2	2	2
Media	2	2	5	2	1	--
Relief-Organizations	3	--	--	1	--	7
Other/Unknown	1	--	--	1	2	1

Bibliography

Adolfo, C., Cruz A., and Alfonso C. (1986), "U.S. Sponsored Contras are Freedom Fighters", in Bender, Bruno, and Szumski (eds.), Opposing Viewpoints: Terrorism, Minnesota, Greenhaven.

Ake, C. (1978), *Revolutionary Pressures in Africa*. London, Zed Press.

Alexander, Y. (1983), "Terrorism and High Technology Weapons," in Freedman, L.Z. and. Alexander, Y. (eds.), Wilmington, Schorlarly Resources.

Alford, R. R. and Friedland, R. (1985), *Powers of Theory*, Cambridge, Cambridge, University Press.

Almond, H.H. (1984), "The Use of Organized Groups by States as Vehicles to Promote their Foreign Policy", in Henry H.H. (ed.), *Terrorism, Political Violence and World Order, Maryland,* University Press of America.

Amin, S. (1974), *Accumulation on a World Scale*. New York, Monthly Review Press.

Amin, S. (1976), *Unequal Development: An Essay on the Social Foundations of Peripheral Capitalism*. New York, Monthly Review Press.

Arkin, W.M. (1997), "The Bomb Has Many Friends", Bulletin of the Atomic Scientists, 63, 36-39.

Bach, R.L. (1980), "On The Holism of a World Systems Perspective", in T. K. Hopkins and Wallerstein, 1. (eds.), *Processes of the World System,* London, Sage.

Baran, P. (1968), *The Political Economy of Growth,* New York, Monthly Review Press.

Baumgartner, T, Walter B. and Burns, T. R. (1975), "Toward a Systems Theory of Unequal Exchange, Uneven Development and Dependency Relations", *Paper Prepared for the Third International Congress of Cybernetics and Systems, Bucharest.*

Begley, S. (1995), "Chain Reaction," in Bender, Bruno, and Szumski, *Urban Terrorism: Current Controversies,* San Diego, Basic Books.

Bekcer, H. S. (1963), *Outsiders: Studies in the Sociology of Deviance,* New York, Free Press.

Bell, B.J. (1975), *Transnational Terror,* California, Hoover Institution on War, Revolution, and Peace.

Benjamin, J. C. (1973), *The Question of Imperialism: The Political Economy of Dominance and Dependence,* New York, Basic Books.

Benzinan, O. (1989), Yitzhak Shamir's Internal Voice, Ha'aretz (February 3).

Bergesen, A. (1980), "Cycles of Formal Colonial Rule", in T. K. Hopkins and Wallerstein,I. (eds.), *Processes of the World System,* London, Sage.

Black, D. (1983), "Crime as Social Control", *American Sociological Review*, 48: 34-45.

Blaw, J. R. and P. M. Blaw (1982), The Cost of Inequality: Metropolitan Structure and Violent Crime, *American Sociological Review,* 47: 114-129.

Bollen, K. (1983), "World System Position, Dependency and Democracy", *American Sociological Review*, 48, 468-479.

Bollen, K. (1977), "Dependency, Population and Development", *Unpublished Manuscript,* Department of Sociology, Brown University.

Bonger, W. A. (1916), Criminality and Economic Conditions, Boston: Little Brown.

Bornschier, V., Chase-Dunn, C. and Rubinson, R. (1978), "Cross-National Evidence of the Effects of Foreign Investment and Aid on Economic Growth and Inequality: A Survey of Findings and a Reanalysis", *American Journal of Sociology*, 84:651- 83.

Braithwaite, J. (1979), *Inequality, Crime and Public Policy,* London, Routledge and Kegan Paul.

Brandt, D. (1985), "Popular Education", in Thomas W.W. (ed.), *Nicaragua: The First Five.* Praeger Publishers, New York.

Brody, R. (1985), Contra Terror in Nicaragua, Boston, South End Press.

Cardoso, F. H. (1977), Consumption of Dependency Theory in the United States", *Latin American Research Review*, 12: 7-24.

Cardoso, F. H. and Faletto, E. (1979), *Dependency and Development in Latin America,* Berkeley, University of California Press.

Chamorro, E. (1986), "U.S. Sponsored Contras are Terrorists", in Bender, Bruno, and Szumski (eds.), *Opposing Viewpoints: Terrorism*, Minnesota, Greenhaven Press.

Charles, L.T. and Jodice, A.D. (1983), *World Handbook of Political and Social Indicators: Political and Government Change*, New Haven, Yale University Press.

Chase-Dunn, C. and Rubinson, R. (1977), "*Toward a Structured Perspective and the World System*", *Politics and Society*, 7:453-476.

Chase-Dunn, C. (1981), "Interstate System and Capitalist World-Economy: One Logic or Two?", in Hollist, W. L., and Rosenari J. N. (eds.), *World System Structure*, London, Sage.

Chilcote, R. H. (1980), "Theories of Dependency: The View from the Periphery", in Ingolf, V. and Anthony R. (eds.), *Dialectics of Third World Development*, New Jersey, Osmund and Co.

Chirot,D. (1977), *Social Change in the Twentieth Century*, New York, Harcourt, Brace and Jovanovich.

Clark, B. (1980), *Technological Terrorism*, Connecticut, Devin-Adair.

Clinard, M. B. and Abbott, D. (1973), *Crime in Developing Countries*, New York, Willey.

Cline, R. S. and Alexander, Y. (1984), *Terrorism: The Soviet Connection*, New York, Crane Russak.

Coleman, S. J (1958), *Nigeria*, Berkeley, University of California Press.

Crayton, W. J. (1983), "Terrorism and the Psychology of the Self", in Freedman L.Z.and Alexander Y. (eds.), *Perspectives on Terrorism*, Wilmington, Scholarly Resources.

Crenshaw, M. (1990), "The Causes of Terrorism", in Kegley, C.W. (ed.), *International Terrorism: Characteristics, Causes, Control*, North Carolina, St. Martin's Press.

Danaher, K. (1984), *In Whose Interest?: A Guide to U.S. South African Relations*, Washington D.C., Institute for Policy Studies.

Danziger, S. and Wheeler, D. (1975), "The Economics of Crime", *Review of Sociological Economy*, 33: 113-31.

Dos Santos, T. (1970), "The Structure of Dependence: Papers and Proceedings", *American Economic Review*, 60: 231-236.

Drar, Y. (1983), "Terrorism as a Challenge to the Democratic Capacity to Govern", in Crenshaw, M. (ed.), *Terrorism, Legitimacy and Power*, New York, St. Martin's Press.

Dupuy, A. (1981), "Feudalism and Slavery: Processes of Uneven Development in France and Saint-Dominique in the Eighteenth Century", *Unpublished Ph.D. Dissertation*, State University of New York at Binghamton.

Ebenstain, W. (1985), *Today's Isms: Communism, Fascism, Capitalism, Socialism*, New Jersey, Prentice Hall.

Eberts, P.I. and Schwirian, K.P. (1969), "Metropolitan Crime Rates and Relative Deprivation", *Criminologica*, 5: 43-52.

Eisenstadt, S. N. (1966), *Modernization: Protest and Change*, New Jersey, Prentice-Hall.

Emmanuel, A. (1972), *Unequal Exchange: A Study of the Imperialism of Trade*, New York, Monthly Press.

Erickson, K. (1966), *Wayward Puritans: A Study in Sociology of Deviance*, New York, John Wily.

Eulau, H. (1967), "Segments of Political Science Most Susceptible to BehavioristicTreatment", in James C.C. (ed.), *Contemporary Political Analysis*, New York, The Free Press.

Evans, P. (1979), *Dependent Development*, New Jersey, Princeton University Press.

Evans, P. and Timberlake, M. (1980), "Dependence, Inequality, and the Growth Of the Tertiary: A Comparative Analysis of Less Developed Countries", *American Sociological Review*, 45:531-552.

Fanon, F. (1962), *The Wretched of the Earth*, New York, Grove Press.

Fanon, F. (1965), A Dying Colonialism, Tr. by Haakon C., Intro. by Adolfo G, New York, Grove Press.

Fanon, F. (1968a), *Black Skin, White Masks*, New York, Grove Press.

Fanon, F. (1968b), *The Wretched of the Earth*, New York, Grove Press.

Fanon, F. (1982), *The Wretched of the Earth*, New York, Grove Press.

Fetter, B. (1979), *Colonial Rule in Africa,* London, The University of Wisconsin Press.

Fieldhouse D. K. (1961), "Imperialism: An Historiographycal Revision", *Economic History*, 14:187-209.

Flemming, P. A., Stohl, M. and Schmid, A. P. (1988), "The Theoretical Utility of Typologies of Terrorism: Lessons and Opportunities" in Stohl, M. (ed.), *The Politics of Terrorism*, New York, Marcel Dekker.

Francis, T.S. (1986), "The Soviet Union Sponsors Terrorism", in Bender, Bruno, and Szumski (eds.), Opposing Viewpoints: Terrorism, Minnesota, Greenhaven Press.

Frank, A. G. (1969), *Underdevelopment or Revolution?*, New York, Monthly Review Press.

Freedman, Z. L. (1983), Terrorism: Problems of the Polistaraxic, Wilmington, Scholarly Resources Inc.

Friedlander, A. R. (1981), *Terrorism and the Law: What Price Safety?*, Gaithersburg, IACP.

Galtung, J. (1971), "A Structural Theory of Imperialism", *Journal of Peace Research*, 8: 81-117.

Gardela, K. and Hoffman, B. (1991), *The RAND Chronology of International Terrorism for 1987,* California, RAND.

Gaucher, N. (1968), *The Terrorists*, London, Secker and Warburg.

Georges-Abeyie, D. E. (1980), "Political Crime and Terrorism", in Newman, G. (ed.), *Crime and Deviance,* California, Sage.

Golan, G. (1990), *Gorbachev's "New Thinking" on Terrorism*. The Washington Papers, Washington, D.C.

Gregor, A. James (1969), The Ideology of Fascism: The Rationale of Totalitarianism. New York, Free Press.

Gregor, A. J. (1983), "Fascism's Philosophy of Violence and the Concept of Terror," in Rapaport, D. C. and Alexander, Y. (eds.), *The Morality of Terrorism: Religious and Secular Justifications*, New York, Pergamond.

Gwinn, P. R. and Goetz, P. W. (1990), The New Encyclopedia Britannica, Vol. 17, Chicago, London, Tokyo.

Hacker, F. J. (1977), *Crusaders, Criminals, Crazies,* New York, Norton.

Hamner, J. and Stanko, E. (1985), "Stripping Away the Rhetoric of Protection: Violence to Women, Law and the State in Britain and the U.S.A", *International Journal of the Sociology of Law*, 13: 357-374.

Harris, D. N. (1914), Intervention and Colonization in Africa, Boston, Houghton Mifflin Company.

Herman, S. E. (1983), *The Real Terror Network: Terrorism in Fact and Propaganda*, Boston, South End Press.

Herman, S. E. (1986), *Soviet-Backed Terrorism is U.S. Propaganda*, in Bander, Bruno, and Szumski (eds.), Opposing Viewpoints: Terrorism, Minnesota, Greenhaven Press.

Herman, S. E. (1987), "U.S. Sponsorship of International Terrorism: An Overview", *Crime and Social Justice*, 27-28: 1-32.

Hobsbawm, E. (1981), *Bandits*, New York, Pantheon Books.

Hobson, J. A. (1938), *Imperialism: A Study*, London, George Allen and Unwin.

Hodgkin, T. (1957), *Nationalism in Colonial Africa*, New York, New York University Press.

Holden, R. T. (1986), "The Contagiousness of Aircraft Hijacking", *American Journal of Sociology*, 91: 874-904.

Hopkins, T. K. and Wallerstein, 1. (1977), "Patterns of Development of the Modern World System", *Sociological Review*, 1: 111-145.

Hout, M. (1979), "Persistent Dependence: The Case of Latin America From Colonial Times to the Present," *Paper Presented at the Annual Meeting of the American Sociological Association*, Boston.

Howe, I. (1975), "The Return of Terror", *Dissert*, 22: 14-21.

Hurz, A. (1987), *Contemporary Trends in World Terrorism*, in Anat K. (ed.), Contemporary Terrorism, Tel Aviv, The Jaffee Center for Strategic Studies.

Hutchinson, M. C. (1973), "The Concept of Revolutionary Terrorism", *Journal Of Conflict Resolution*, 6: 338-341.

Hutchinson, M.C. (1978), *Revolutionary Terrorism: The FLN in Algeria, 1954-1962*, California, Hoover Institution Press.

Hyans, E. (1974), *Terrorists and Terrorism*, New York, St. Martin's Press.

Inkeles, A. (1975), "Becoming Modern: Individual Change in Six Developing Countries", *Ethos*, 3: 323-342.

Jackman, R. W. (1975), *Politics and Social Inequality: A Comparative Analysis*, New York, Wiley.

Jackman, R. W. (1982), "Dependence on Foreign Investment and Economic Growth in the Third World", *World Politics*, 34: 175196.

Jaffe, H. (1985), *A History of Africa*, London, Zed Books.

Jenkins, B. (1975), *International Terrorism: A New Mode of Conflict*, Los Angeles, Crescent.

Jenkins, B. (1998), "Will Terrorists go Nuclear? A Reappraisal", in Kushner, H.W. (ed.), *The Future of Terrorism: Violence in the New Millennium*, London, Sage.

Jones, R.W. (1987), "The Religious Legitimation of Counterviolence, Insights From Latin American Liberation Theology", in Kliever, D. O. (ed.),

The Terrible Meek: Religion and Revolution in Cross-Cultural Perspective, New York, Paragon House Publishers.

Kellett, A. (1981), *International Terrorism: A Retrospective and Prospective Examination*, Ottawa, Canadian Department of National Defense.

Kick, E. L. and Lafree, G. (1985), "Development and the Social Context of Murder and Theft", *Comparative Social Research*, 8: 37-58.

Kirkham, P. J. (1969), *Assassination and Political Violence*, Washington, D.C., Government Printing Office.

Kushner, H.W. (1998), *The Future of Terrorism: Violence in the new Millennium*, London, Sage.

Laqueur, W. (1977), *Terrorism*, Boston, Little Brown.

Laqueur, W. (1987), *The Age of Terrorism*, Boston, Little Brown.

Legun, C. (1981), *Annual, Africa Contemporary Record: Annual Survey and Documents*, New York, Africana Publishing Corporation.

Lemert, M. E. (1951), *Social Pathology*, New York, McGraw-Hill.

Lenin, V.1. (1966), *Imperialism: The Highest Stage of Capitalism*, London, Bantam Books.

Leventhal, P.L. (1992), *"Plugging the Leaks in Nuclear Export Controls: Why Bother?"*, in Bender, Bruno, and Szumski (eds.), Opposing Viewpoints: Terrorism, Minnesota, Greenhaven.

Levine, V. (1971), *The Cameroon Federal Republic*, New York, Cornell University Press.

Lilly, J. R., Cullen, P. T., and Ball, R. A. (1989), *Criminological Theory: Context and Consequences*, London, Sage.

Linear, M. (1985), *Zapping the Third World*, London, Pluto Press.

Lipsey, R. and Blomstrom, M. (1986), *Firm Size and Foreign Direct Investment*, New York, National Bureau of Economic Research.

Lisker, J. (1986), "Terrorists and Guerrillas in Africa", in Tavin, E. and Alexander, A. (eds.), *Terrorists or Freedom Fighters*, Virginia, Hero Books.

Livingstone, N. C., and Arnold, T. E. (1986), *Fighting Back: Winning the War Against Terrorism*, Massachusetts, Lexington Books.

Lodge, J. (1981), *Terrorism: A Challenge to the State*, Oxford, Martin Robertson.

Lynch, M. J. and Groves, B. W. (1990), *A Primer in Radical Criminology*, New York, Harrow and Heston.

Magubane, B. (1987), "South Africa: The Dialectic of Oppression and Resistance", in Turok, B. (ed.), *Africa's Crisis*, London, Institute for African Alternatives.

Marighela, C. (1971), *Minimanaul of the Urban Guerrilla*, New York, Penguin.

Martin, L.J. (1990), "The Media's Role in Terrorism", in Kegley, C.W. (ed.), *International Terrorism: Characteristics, Causes, Control*, North Carolina, St. Martin's Press.

May, W. P. (1974), "Terrorism As Strategy and Ecstasy", *Social Research*, 41: 277-198.

Mazrui, A. A. and Tidy, M. (1984), *Nationalism and New States in Africa*, Ibadan, Heineman.

Mendelson, J. (1992), "Dismantling the Arsenals: Arms Control and the New World Agenda", *The Brookings Review*, Spring.

Memmi, A. (1965), *The Colonizer and the Colonized*, New York, Orion Press.

Merkl, P. (1986), *Political Violence and Terror*, Berkeley, University of California Press.

Messner, F. S. (1980), "Income Inequality and Murder Rates: Some Cross-National Findings", *Comparative Social Research*, 3: 185-198.

Micholus, F. (1981), *Combating International Terrorism: A Quantitative Analysis, Ph.D. Dissertation,* (Yale University).

Miller, W. B. (1974), "Ideology and Criminal Justice Policy", in Reasons, C. E. (ed.), *Criminology: Crime and Criminals*, California, Goodyear.

Mitchell, H. T. (1985), *Politically Motivated Terrorism in North America: The Threat and the Response*, Unpublished Ph.D. Dissertation, Carleton University.

Modelski, G. (1978), "The Long Cycle of Global Politics and the Nation State", *Comparative Studies in Society and History,* 20: 214-235.

Mondlane, E. (1969), *The Struggle for Mozambique*, Baltimore, Penguin.

Mongo, B. (1970), *King Lazarus,* London, Heineman.

Moss, R. (1972), *The Way for the Cities*, New York, Cowand, McCann and Geoghegan.

Motley, J. B. (1981), "International Terrorism: A New Mode of Warfare", *International Security Review*, 6: 93-123.

Moughrabi, F. (1992), "Israeli Control and Palestinian Resistance", *Social Justice,* 19: 46-62.

National Advisory Committee on Criminal Justice Standards and Goals, Law EnforcementAssistant Agency, *Disorders and Terrorism.* (1976), Washington, D.C., U.S. Government Printing Office.

Newman, G. R. and Lynch, M. J. (1987), "From Feuding to Terrorism: The Ideology of Vengence", *Contemporary Crises,* 11: 223-242.

Newman, W. L. and Berger, R. J. (1988), "Competing Perspectives on Cross-National Crime: An Evaluation of Theory and Evidence. *The Sociological Quarterly,* 2: 281-313.

Nkrumah, K. (1968), *The Last Stage of Imperialism*, London, Heinemann.

Nolan, P. D. (1983), "Status in the World System, Income Inequality, and Economic Growth", *American Journal of Sociology*, 89: 410-419.

Nyong'o, P. A. (1986), *Military Intervention in African Politics*, Colorado, Westview Press.

Ohaegbulam, P. U. (1977), *Nationalism in Colonial and Post-Colonial Africa,* Washington, D.C., University Press of America.

Okwodiba N. (1985), *Africa: The Political Challenge*, Presidential Address to the Sixth Biannual Meeting of the African Association of Political Science, Africa Hall, Addis Ababa, Ethiopia.

O'Malley, P. (1980), "The Class Production of Crime: Banditry and Class Strategies in England and Australia", *Research in Law and Society*, 3: 181-99.

Parry, A. (1976), *Terrorism From Robespierre to Arafat*, New York, The Vanguard Press.

Pepinsky, E. and Quinney, R. (1991), *Criminology as Peacemaking*, Indiana, University Press.

Perdue, W. D. (1986), *Sociological Theory: Explanation, Paradigm, and Ideology*, California, Mayfield Publishers.

Perdue, W. D. (1989), *Terrorism and the State: A Critique of Domination Through Fear*, New York, Prager.

Pfost, R. D. (1984), "State Terrorist on a Global Scale: The Role of Israel", *Crime and Social Justice*, 21-22: 58-80.

Pfost, R. D. (1987), "Reagan's Nicaragua Policy: A Case Study of Political Deviance and Crime", *Crime and Social Justice*, 28: 66-87.

Pieterse, J. N. (1987), "The Washington-Tel-Aviv Connection: Global Frontier Management", *Crime and Justice*, 27-28: 201-219.

Pluchinsky, J. (1982), "Political Terrorism in Western Europe: Some Themes and Variations", in Alexander, J. and Myers, K. A. (eds.), *Terrorism in Europe*, New York, St. Martin's Press.

Poland, J. M. (1988), *Understanding Terrorism: Groups, Strategies, and Responses*, New Jersey, Prentice Hall.

Portes, A. (1976), "On the Sociology of National Development: Theories and Issues", *American Journal of Sociology*, 82: 555-585.

Prebisch, R. (1950), *The Economic Development of Latin America and its Principal Problems*, New York, United Nations Department of Social and Economic Affairs.

Qureshi, S. (1976), "Political Violence in the South Asian Subcontinent", in Alexander, Y. (ed.), *International Terrorism: Regional and Global Perspectives*, New York, Praeger.

Rapoport, D.C. (1990), "Religion and Terror: Thugs, Assassins, and Zealots", in Kegley, C.W. (ed.), *International Terrorism Characteristics, Causes, Control*, North Carolina, St. Martin's Press.

Reagan, R. (1985), *The New Network of Terrorist States*, An Address to the American Bar Association, Washington, D.C.

Rodney, W. (1982), *How Europe Underdeveloped Africa*, Washington, D.C., Howard University Press.

Rubenstein, R. E. (1990), "The Non-Cause of Terrorism", in Kegley, C. W. (ed.), *International Terrorism: Characteristics, Causes, Control*, North Carolina, St. Martin's Press.

Rubinson, R. (1976), "The World Economy and the Distribution of Income Within States: A Cross-National Study", *American Sociological Review*, 41: 638-659.

Rubinson, R. and Quinlan, D. (1977), "Democracy and Social Inequality: A Reanalysis", *American Sociological Review*, 42: 611-622.

Rubinson, T. D. and London, B. (1991), "Dependency, Inequality, and Political Violence: A Cross-National Analysis", *Journal of Political and Military Sociology*, 19: 119-156.

Rushworth, M. K. (1990), "Why Modern Terrorism? Three Causes Springing from the Seeds of the 1960s", in Kegley, C.W. (ed.), *International Terrorism: Characteristics, Causes, Control*, North Carolina, St. Martin's Press.

Schlagheck, M. D. (1990), "The Superpowers, Foreign Policy, and Terrorism", in Kegley, W. C. (ed.), *International Terrorism: Characteristics, Causes, Control*, North Carolina, St. Martin's Press.

Schmid, A. P. and de Graaf J. (1982), *Violence as Communication: Insurgent Terrorism and the Western News Media*, Beverly Hills, Sage.

Schmid, A. P. (1983), *Political Terrorism: A Research Guide to Concepts, Theories, Data Bases and Literature*, Amsterdam, North Roland Publishing Company.

Shank, G. (1984), "Counterterrorism and Foreign Policy", *Crime and Social Justice*, 27: 33-65.

Shelley, L. 1. (1985), "American Crime: An International Anomaly?", *Comparative Social Research*, 8: 81-96.

Shultz, R. (1978), "Conceptualizing Political Terrorism: A Typology", *Journal of International Affairs*, 32: 31-49.

Skocpol, T. (1977), "Wallerstein's World Capitalist System: A Theoretical and Historical Critique", *American Journal of Sociology*, 82: 1075-1090.

Skocpol, T. (1979), *States and Social Revolutions*, Cambridge, Cambridge University Press.

Smith, N. (1984), *Uneven Development: Nature, Capital and the Production of Space*, New York, Basil Blackwell.

Sobel, A.L. (1975), *Political Terrorism*, New York, Facts on File, Inc.

Sokolski, H. D. (1992), "Statement to the U.S. Senate Committee on Governmental Affairs", in Bender, Bruno, and Szumski (eds.), *Nuclear Proliferation: Opposing View Points*, California, Greenhaven Press.

Sterling, C. (1981), *The Terror Network*, New York, Holt, Rinehart and Winston.

Stohl, M. and Lopez, G. (1984), *The State as Terrorist*, Westport, Greenwood Press.

Stohl, M. (1988), "Demystifying Terrorism: The Myths and Realities of Contemporary Political Terrorism", in Stohl, M. (ed.), *The Politics of Terrorism*, New York, Marcel Decker.

170 Globalization of Terrorism

Swedenborg, B. (1979), *The Multinational Operations of Swedish Firms: An Analysis of Determinants and Effects*, Stockholm, Industriens Utrednungsintitut.

Sweitzer, G. E and Dorsch, C. C. (1998), *Superterrorism: Assasins, Mobsters, and Weapons of Mass Destruction,* New York, Plenum Trade.

Sydney Morning Herald (1986), "U.S. Takes Steps to Isolate Syria", Sydney Australia, October, 29.

Tannenbaum, F. (1938), *Crime and the Community,* New York, Columbia University Press.

Taylor, L. C. and David, J. A. (1983), *World Handbook of Political and Social Indicators: Cross-National Attributes and Rates of Change,* New Haven, Yale University Press.

Thornton, P. T. (1964), "Terror as a Weapon of Political Agitation", in Eckstein, H. (ed.), *Internal War,* New York, Free Press.

Tilly, C. (1978), *From Mobilization to Revolution,* Reading, Addison-Wesley.

Timberlake, M. (1984), *Urbanization in the World Economy,* New York, Academic Press.

Turk, A. (1984), "Political Crime", in Meier, R. P. (ed.), *Major Forms of Crime,* California, Sage.

Uku-Wertimer, S. (1988), *Contemporary Africa and Political Leaders*, Massachusetts, Copley Publishing Group.

U.S. Air Force Special Operations School, Hurlburt Field, Florida, July1985.

United States Department of State (1981), *Current Policy No. 258,* Alexander Haig, News Conference, January, 28.

United Nations Center on Transnational Corporations (1988), *Transnational Corporations in World Development,* New York, United Nations.

Ustinov, G (1986), "Afghan Rebels are Terrorists", in Bender, Bruno, and Szumski (eds.), *Opposing Viewpoints,* Minnesota, Greenhaven Press.

Vetter, H. J. and Perlstein, G. R. (1991), *Perspectives on Terrorism*, California, Brooks and Cole Publishing Company.

Waggoner, F. E. (1980), *Dragon Rouge: The Rescue of Hostages in the Congo,* Washington, D.C., U.S. Government Printing Office.

Walker, T. W. (1982), *Nicaragua in Revolution,* New York, Praeger.

Wallerstein, I. (1974), *The Modern World System,* New York, Academic Press.

Wallerstein, I. (1979a), *The Capitalist World Economy,* London, Cambridge University Press.

Wallerstein, I. (1979b), "Class Formation in the Capitalist World Economy", in Wallerstein, I. (ed.), *The Capitalist World Economy,* Cambridge, Cambridge, University Press.

Wallerstein, I. (1980), *The Modern World System 11: Mercantilism and the Consolidation of the European World Economy,* New York, Academic Press.

Wallerstein, L. (1982), "The Rise and Future Demise of the World Capitalist System: Concepts for Comparative Analysis", in Ham, A. and Shanin, T. (eds.),

Introduction to the Sociology of Developing Societies, New York, Monthly Review Press.

Wallerstein, I. (1989), *The Modern World System III: The Second Great Expansion of the Capitalist World Economy,* New York, Academic Press.Walter, E. V. (1969), *Terrorism and Resistance: A Study of Political Violence,* New York, Oxford University Press.

Walton, J. (1982), "The International Economy and Peripheral Urbanization", in Fainstein N.1. and Feinstein S.S. (eds.), *Urban Policy Under Capitalism,* Beverley Hills, Sage.

Wardlaw, G. (1939), *Political Terrorism,* New York, Cambridge University Press.

Wardlaw, G. (1988), "Terror as an Instrument of Foreign Policy", in Rapoport, D.C. (ed.), *Inside Terrorist Organizations,* New York, Columbia University Press.

Weede, E. (1980), "Beyond Misspecification in Sociological Analyses of Income Inequality", *American Sociological Review,* 45:497-501.

Wheeler, J. (1986), "Afghan Rebels are Freedom Fighters", in Bender, Bruno, and Szumski (eds.), *Opposing Viewpoints: Terrorism,* Minnesota, Greenhaven Press.

White, J. R. (1998), *Terrorism: An Introduction,* California, West.

Wilkinson, P. (1973), "Three Questions on Terrorism, Government and Opposition", Vol. 6, No. 3, Summer.

Wilkinson, P. (1976), *Political Terrorism,* London, MacMillan.

Wilkinson, P. (1977), *Terrorism and the Liberal State,* London, MacMillan.

Wilkinson, P. (1979), *Terrorism and the Liberal State,* New York, University Press.

Wilkinson, P. (1990), "The Sources of Terrorism: Terrorists' Ideologies and Beliefs", in Kegley, C.W. (ed.), *International Terrorism: Characteristics, Causes, Control,* North Carolina, St. Martin's Press.

Wright, J. W. (1984), "Terrorism: A Mode of Warfare", *Military Review,* 10, 35-45.